# GOD
## TOUCHES

# GOD
# TOUCHES

## FINDING FAITH
## *in the* CRACKS
## *and* SPACES *of my* LIFE

## DAN GILLIAM

**Standard**®
PUBLISHING
*Bringing The Word to Life*
Cincinnati, Ohio

*To* CHARLIE *and* ANN

Thank you for giving me your best.

Published by Standard Publishing, Cincinnati, Ohio
www.standardpub.com

© 2007 Dan C. Gilliam

Project editor: Laura Derico
Cover and interior design: Scott Ryan

All Scripture quotations, unless otherwise indicated, are taken from the HOLY BIBLE, NEW INTERNATIONAL VERSION®. NIV®. Copyright © 1973, 1978, 1984 by International Bible Society. Used by permission of Zondervan. All rights reserved. Scripture marked *The Message* is taken from *The Message*. Copyright © 1993, 1994, 1995, 1996, 2000, 2001, 2002. Used by permission of NavPress Publishing Group.

ISBN 978-0-7847-1963-3

13 12 11 10 09 08 07        9 8 7 6 5 4 3 2 1

Library of Congress Cataloging-in-Publication Data
Gilliam, Dan C., 1959-
  God touches : finding faith in the cracks and spaces of life / Dan C.
Gilliam.
     p. cm.
  ISBN 0-7847-1963-2 (perfect bound)
  1. Spirituality. I. Title.
BV4501.3.G558 2007
231.7--dc22
                                                  2006037312

If we want to hear God we have to listen, and yet the one deficiency epidemic among adults is listening. We don't listen. We won't listen. We are willing to do almost anything to keep ourselves from listening.

**Mike Yaconelli**
*Dangerous Wonder: The Adventure of Childlike Faith*

# CONTENTS

# ACKNoWLEDGMENTS

Sometime around 1998, my wife, Lynn, and I sold everything we owned and piled into a 21-foot 1975 Dodge motor home. It was not much more than a glorified van with a single bed, small stove, tiny sink, and compact toilet, but it was home and we loved it. This would be the first of three times (so far) that we liquidated our meager estate and hit the road with more of a journey in mind than a destination. Driven by a need for simplicity and a desire to see the country at road's-eye view, we launched out with a few hundred dollars, a flimsy plan for earning income along the way, and a strong reliance upon the God of the universe.

At our North Carolina going away party, one of our friends gave me a T-shirt that appropriately read, "Not all who wander are lost." This and a bumper sticker that identified us as "Friends of Bill W." characterized our mission to experience life, art, and the boundaries of American adventure. Jack Kerouac, J. D. Salinger, Charles Kuralt, William Least-Heat Moon, Garrison Keillor, Anne Lamott, and Carrie Fisher, among others, guided our imaginations with their inspired writings. Friends new and old encouraged us to follow our bliss so that they could live vicariously through us. Stray cats and homeless people wanted to live with us. It was a wild and magical time.

Making our daily bread by playing music and selling handmade jewelry and original art, Lynn and I found no lack of churches in the southern and midwestern states interested in hearing songs and stories from the poor, free-spirited gypsies we were becoming. And while the income opportunities got fewer and thinner the farther west we traveled, we nevertheless pressed on to enjoy in leisurely fashion the people and places we were encountering. Somewhere in Oklahoma, our paths crossed the first of several people we would meet who were crossing the country on foot. Walking Tom, as he referred to himself, had left the West Coast and was heading east at a relatively fast clip until he got bogged down (his words) in his travels by a young woman with whom he was infatuated. She would later join Tom on his U.S. walking tour and become Mrs. Walking Tom somewhere around Mississippi. Anyway, it was Tom who introduced me to portable e-mail technology, via PocketMail, allowing me to document my journeys and perspectives that eventually became the book you are about to read.

As Lynn and I found various stopping points over the years in places such as Nashville, Tennessee, Durango, Colorado, Cottage Grove, Oregon, Roanoke, Virginia, and Hatteras, North Carolina (twice), we garnered new friendships and experiences that inevitably impacted my story-writing and tale-telling. Since 1999, I have had a small but devoted following of friends and family who have read with interest my ramblings, grumblings, travelogues, and diatribes. With each e-mail posting for a list that began as Really Cool Jesus People (after one of my songs) and later became Paint Your Life, I received encouragement to put all of these stories together in a book. To all of these beautiful people and for all of these wonderful places I will be eternally grateful, and I carry them in my heart. The life touches they gave me became the God touches I wrote about. Because of their love and influence I will never be the same, which is a good thing. Though my appreciation for them runs much deeper than this simple, sweeping acknowledgment, this is my official thanks to all who have had a hand in shaping my life, my art, and my first book. Chances are you already know that I love you. Let me know what I can do for you. Blessings on your journey.

Dan Gilliam
www.dangilliam.net
Longmont, Colorado

# INTRODUCTION

I grew up in a church whose theology was so narrow that not only were all of "them" going to Hell, many of "us" thought we were probably headed there too. Having heard so many sermons and stories about people suffering in the unquenchable flames of eternal punishment (many of whom were there because I didn't tell them what I knew about the love of Jesus), I didn't get a good night's sleep from kindergarten until I drank my first bottle of wine at age fifteen. Though I was as good a kid as any, due to my curious constitution and appetite for adventure, I never felt like I measured up to the religious standards that were meted out with urgency and regularity from the sanctuary pulpit to the Sunday school flannelgraph board. Every night, I knelt by my bed and asked Jesus to forgive my sins, naming them one by one, knowing in my heart that I was forgetting something that God would remember and punish me for when the time was right. I was confident Jesus would come like a thief in the night when I least expected it and steal back my soul because it was marred by sin. Somehow I had missed the point that it was my very inability to be flawlessly obedient that had led Christ to make the supreme sacrifice on my behalf in the first place. It would be years before I would fully believe and accept this gospel of grace. I know many Christ-followers who are still working hard on this.

Almost everyone I have met in my lifetime grew up with some kind of religious influence in his or her home. Only a small percentage of these people transitioned through puberty and into adulthood without some kind of faith-shaking or religion-altering experience. I once lived in Oregon for two years and met an unusually large number of people who claimed to have no belief in God, at least not in a defined supreme being that cared about them or influenced the events in their lives. Interestingly enough, among this fun, loving, and intriguing community of self-proclaimed witches, pagans, Buddhists, and fairies (and combinations thereof), almost all had a Christian background of some sort and were in the process of rejecting this faith. They had not yet completely worked out what it was that would replace their childhood beliefs, but they were certain that they wanted neither what their parents had nor what the popular voices of mainstream evangelicalism were preaching. And they were willing to go to any lengths to find something different, even if they had to create their own cross-pollinated, hybrid, pseudo religion. While they weren't sure what to call it, they were very committed to their antireligious religion and ironically, were evangelistic about it.

To be sure, in these ever-widening circles of spirituality seekers, *mystic* is a much cooler label than *Methodist*, and *Buddhist* is hipper than *Baptist* any day. Among the younger generations, Christianity—as a term and a religion—has a hard time of it these days. Though it may be popular to wander from original systems of belief in search of more palatable perspectives on spirituality and more user-friendly interpretations of truth, it is apparent that many of these searchers stand to come full circle. Eventually. These spiritual gypsies wander back a few at a time to the familiar communities and campfires around which they first heard God songs and Jesus stories, bringing with them a deep commitment to their faith and a rich testimony of change. Primitive cultures, as well as the American Amish, are known to have encouraged and even forced their adolescents to venture out and explore the unknown, testing their new experiences against that which they have learned from the elders and families of their tribe. If we believe Proverbs 22:6, then we can "train a child in the way he should go, and when he is old he will not turn from it." This means that those of us who have parented and discipled children well will have nothing to fear when the curious, the disenchanted, and even the disturbed youngster leaves the nest to test his wings and try her truth, through whatever means necessary to affirm his or her faith. Though we might prefer to protect our loved ones from painful experiences, I doubt that any of us would choose to have robots for children—incapable of thinking original thoughts or making personal decisions.

I have been around long enough to see that, though not everyone has to lose his or her faith in order to find it, there seems to be a significant number of us out here in the high desert plains who need some kind of jolt to our souls—either by design, default, or destiny—which can assist us in finding a grounded belief that we can own. Something has to separate us from our faith so that we can find it again and embrace it as we would a new and shiny Christmas toy. It appears to be a time-tested fact that, one way or another, the faith of our mothers and fathers eventually leaves us wanting; to be spiritually satisfied every individual must establish or at least stumble upon his or her own personal relationship with God.

The problem is that while the spiritual juices never stop flowing, and God never stops touching their lives, many people during a period of spiritual disconnectedness think that if they are not regularly going to church, they are outside the realm of Christ contact and are in grave danger of eternal hellfire. Though no one would care to admit it, they believe that God's grace is somehow activated by the sound of one's seat sliding across a waxed, wooden pew and preserved by semi-regular acts of confession, or occasional encounters with a single-serve portion of grape juice and mini-crackers. Even though they have years of prayer, faith, and Christian dedication under their belts, some sadly believe that Christ is automatically thrown out with the holy water. With no worship service to keep them in the loop of God's kingdom, an extended lapse in church attendance somehow makes all former faithfulness null and void in God's eyes.

Far too many people think that Christ cannot be found outside the traditional or modern modes of organized Christianity.

It is this limited and exclusive perspective on faith that fuels the postmodern's process of searching for a God idea and practice that includes anything but the much-maligned person or teachings of Jesus Christ. According to my experience and that of a myriad God-seekers in our communities, finding Christ is not as difficult as we have been told.

For those open to the work of the Spirit and the influence of God, Jesus Christ is actively seeking and saving the lost—making himself known through all sorts of random acts of kindness and senseless acts of beauty. He is everywhere and in all things, available to any who would reach out with an open mind and a willing heart. Anyone with a hungry soul capable of sampling the delicious work of God in this world can be touched, even changed, by the life and work of Christ, whether that person realizes it or not. The church, local and universal, is nothing more or less than the body of Christ; a mass of struggling hoi polloi saved by grace, much larger and more all encompassing than any of us dare to imagine. The apostle Paul testified to this when he wrote:

> For by him all things were created: things in heaven and on earth, visible and invisible, whether thrones or powers or rulers or authorities; all things were created by him and for him. He is before all things and in him all things hold together. And he is the head of the body, the church; he is the beginning and the firstborn from among the dead, so that in everything he might have the supremacy. For God was pleased to have all his fullness dwell in him, and through him to reconcile to himself all things, whether things on earth or things in heaven, by making peace through his blood, shed on the cross. (Colossians 1:16-20)

From what I have seen, many who in evangelical circles are labeled "lost" or "seekers" are simply those who have grown up or are growing up with the Truth and are in the process of determining whether they want to believe it and embrace it for themselves. On God's timeline they are not losing their salvation as many fear, but rather, inching closer to a more authentic salvation through their intentional and independent assault on what's out there. I personally know many adults possessing a mature faith who were once chronic backsliders, and whose names regularly appeared on prayer lists of the sick, suffering, and hell-bound. I myself am one. By God's mercy we are allowed to survive ourselves in more than one season of debauchery, finding our prodigal way home to drink again from the inexhaustible springs of living water. One day at a time, we walk upright in the light and love of a functioning relationship with God, enjoying a life full of kindred spirits with whom we share our journeys. We who have traveled these treacherous paths understand that there can be no regretting the past or wishing to change it. It is this very trail of tears that has brought us to the place of usefulness and happiness that otherwise may not have existed for us. And although it may have been painful for those who loved us to witness, they can now testify that our misguided meandering was well worth the heartache.

It is from this perspective of turning from and returning to faith that I have written this book. For it is on this precipice past the mountains of despair, on this plateau beyond the canyons of discouragement, that I have climbed to be able to observe God at work in all aspects of life. I claim no power to do the right thing—only an absurd ability to trust God and see the good in hardship, as well as the beauty in creation. Though there are more spiritual connecting points and experiences than can be written in one book, and maybe even in one lifetime, I have documented here some of the ways in which I have seen and felt the touch of God upon my own heart.

I wrote this book for the man who no longer believes that his best or only encounter with God can happen while his body sits stiffly in a church pew; his spirit longing to be hiking in the woods with his dog. I wrote it for the college student who is discovering the freedom to explore and express fresh perspectives on God, anxious to know that God does not condemn him for using his mind. This book is for the woman who has no friends to whom she can confess that her truest expression of gratitude and loving worship to her maker occurs when listening to a jazz CD or grooming her cat. This book is for the artist, the athlete, the gardener, the physician, the mechanic, the teacher, and the pilot who touch the Spirit every day but aren't sure how to celebrate these encounters beyond the confines of their religious practices, unable to admit that they are their purest and most honest experiences of God. Last but certainly not least, this book is for the pastor, the priest, or the rabbi who ministers daily to the hurting and confused—all the while thirsty for fresh brushes with the Maker who can rejuvenate the soul and prolong a career, or maybe even a life.

This collection of God encounters is personal and individual, yet universal in application. Without my own turn from and return to faith in the God of the Bible, the Jesus of the empty tomb, and the Holy Spirit of Pentecost, I would not currently enjoy these daily spiritual happenings. Moreover, without the inconceivable life and boundless work of Jesus Christ, I would not have experienced God's work in my life long before I was ready again to call myself a Christ-follower and participate fully in the life of a local church. It will be my delight to learn of the man, woman, or child who upon reading these words stopped to sip the wine of grace in his or her own simple, everyday, ordinary, and extraordinary life experiences. And perhaps they will in time, as I have, lift their faces to worship the radiant and risen Christ, and see a bigger picture of his work in this luscious and wonderful world.

# (1)

# CREATIVE WRITING

## BUZZ CUTS,
## BANK ROBBERS,
### *and the*
## BIG CHIEF

If we turn to the most intense experiences of our past—in this case, peak experiences—we find that they bring us alive. As writers, we depend on these experiences to give us our most vivid emotions, images, tensions, and meaning. It is no wonder that the novelists whose works endure and continue to move us even centuries later are often accused of drawing their imagery and their "fictional" situations from real life.

**Hal Zina Bennett**
*Write from the Heart*

I t all began for me in the second grade. My knack for spinning a yarn and telling a tall tale, which often landed me in the hot seat at home and church, came in handy when it was time to write a story for Mrs. Shepherd's class. Armed with a No. 2 pencil and my Big Chief wide-lined writing tablet, I was, at least in my own mind, a fiction force with which to be reckoned. While my classmates turned in feeble narratives about pet tricks or their parents' careers, I wrote matter-of-factly about Earth-visiting Martians and their backyard scientific experiments on my dog and me. It was with great earnestness that I cranked out descriptive accounts of running away from home to join the rodeo (I always wanted to compete in the greased pig contest) and of praying a road-kill turtle back from the dead. And I had witnesses, even if they were in kindergarten and I paid them off with Tootsie Rolls.

I told these and other stories with such a convincing flare that, in trying to persuade my reader of their reality, I came to believe in them myself. I could be mistaken, but I think the gist of my second grade teacher's conference with my parents was my overactive imagination and the concern that if I were to continue in this direction, I might later run into trouble distinguishing between fact and fairy tale. Truth is, Mrs. Shepherd was right. Even now as I recount this chapter of my life, I may very well be embellishing. Be what it may, near the end of my second year of school I was lovingly admonished to write stories that could be documented by adult members of my family or community. Though this could have been a wet blanket thrown onto my young, creative mind, it did not prove to be much of a problem at all. Real life, in my little world, has always been at least as interesting as any fiction I could ever write.

As a young lad I must have also been stricken with an advanced case of vanity, for there can be no other explanation for the fits I threw when it came time to go to the barbershop. What with the older kids starting to wear longer hair, due mostly to the British pop invasion of America, I wanted more than anything to grow out a mop-top-type hairdo like the Beatles, the Rolling Stones, and Herman's Hermits. But my dad would hear none of it. No son of his was going to turn out to be a dope-smoking hippie like that long-haired neighbor boy who drove his hot rod Barracuda all over town with his hussy hip-hugger-wearing girlfriend riding shotgun. No sir. Until that discussion, I had no idea that the length of one's hair contributed so heavily to his or her detrimental conduct. But according to many well-informed adults at that time, long hair was a sign of rebellion and disrespect. After all, the Bible does say that those who don long hair should be ashamed of themselves. Or something like that. All I know is that the Indian pictured on my Big Chief writing pad had long hair and he didn't look ashamed of anything.

Regardless of how we felt, the default haircut for '60s kids like me, with former military men for dads, was the classic "pineapple" buzz cut. This was the style most hated and feared by the young males of my space race generation, in spite of the fact that the cut was made famous by the astronauts themselves. Truth was, any fresh haircut for a boy in grade school in those days was an invitation to ridicule and harassment that bordered on torture. Name-calling, note-passing, head-slapping and even playground butt-whuppings were standard fare for the kid with the fresh "whitewalls," especially if he had previously participated in the pineapple torture of others.

It was a perpetual cycle that didn't end until fourth or fifth grade. By then, we were all wearing a longer cut with a side part, using Vitalis to keep the cowlicks down, and dousing ourselves with Avon cologne that came in car- and football-shaped bottles. Some of us even put cologne on our hair, just in case it was cool and we didn't know it. Johnny Unitas was the NFL poster man for the pineapple cut, which is probably the main reason the Baltimore Colts lost Super Bowl III to the New York Jets, as predicted by Joe Namath. Broadway Joe, on the other hand, sported a side-part haircut and did TV commercials for Vitalis and other men's grooming products, which for some reason featured many beautiful women. Message conveyed: the pineapple buzz cut was not the haircut to wear if you wanted to meet women.

My creative writing took on a new dimension in 1967 as national and world events began to heat up. I had no shortage of true stories about which to write that year and had to turn to shoplifting to keep myself supplied with Big Chiefs. (Note: I was caught red-handed with three Butterfinger bars in my pocket three days after my Christian baptism. And though it would have made a very interesting story for class and even Sunday school, I decided not to write about this incident in the interest of personal reputation.) My inspiration for at least one such story came the day my sisters and I had front row seats to a criminal FBI capture in our tiny Missouri town. Much to the later shock of our parents, we sat glued to our swing set seats as rifle-toting federal agents wearing brown, government-issue hats (probably to cover their pineapple cuts) moved in to arrest a band of bank robbers who rented the house next door to us. I remember having mixed feelings about seeing one of the men handcuffed facedown in his grassy knoll of a front yard while a helicopter circled overhead like a vulture eyeing its dying dinner. I felt like I knew them, not so much because we had ever talked, though we had exchanged a few winks and Goober Pyle-like clicks. This vague sense of familiarity likely came from the rainy-day hours my sisters and I watched from our covered patio as the younger guy and girl bank robbers engaged in window-fogging make out sessions in the backseat of their alleged getaway car. This made them celebrities in our eyes and way more interesting than our regular, boring neighbors—one of whom was the barber.

Much to our (and their) embarrassment, one day our mom caught on to us (and them) and marched over to knock on their backseat window to give them an unasked-for piece of her mind. She informed the surprised, steamed-up couple that her Ivory-pure children were just yards away, straining on tiptoes to get any glimpse of the amorous wrestling match. I don't recall the Bonnie and Clyde wannabes' reaction, but my mom most likely dragged my sisters and me into the house by our dislocated shoulders. It may very well have been in response to this confrontation that my outlaw neighbors went out and robbed a bank.

It was under this same carport that my younger sisters and I heatedly debated whether men had it worse because they had to go fight in Vietnam or women had a tougher time of it because they had to endure the pains of childbirth. It was an ancient debate: War versus Motherhood. My point was that I'd rather go to war any day than have a baby. I still feel pretty strongly about that. Of course, I had a history of playing with toy guns, which gave me a false sense of what war was about and a soft idea of what it meant to kill somebody. In our childhood wars, where one boy representing G. I. Joe could do battle with another kid playing John Wayne, you could always get another life by simply saying "You missed me" if you didn't want the battlefield cries of "I got you" or "You're dead" to be true. Along the same lines, the only firsthand knowledge my sisters had of motherhood was in making sure their Betsy Wetsy had a high enough water level so she could wet her diapers when squeezed. Babies came from boxes on Christmas morning, and taking care of them meant turning them right side up to make them stop crying. Neither my three sisters nor I had any idea about that which we talked so authoritatively. But it made good writing medicine for Big Chief.

In my high school years, creative writing as a subject matter and as an extracurricular activity proved to be too burdensome for my lifestyle. Some of my adolescent hurts had turned into rebellion, and I found studying to be too difficult to juggle with smoking pot and listening to Black Sabbath and Pink Floyd through headphones. Forced to make a choice, I decided quite painlessly that school had to go. But rather than give up my love for writing, I simply quit working at it so hard and instead submitted to the creative stream that flowed without inhibition from my THC- and LSD-liberated mind. Though I failed to acknowledge the potential for brain damage, I embraced the beat-freak identity that accompanied writing love poems and protest songs. Frequently performing my original scribblings impromptu at bonfires, talent shows, and keg parties, I discovered new motivation for creative writing: free love and easy money. This discovery temporarily kept me from the encumbrances of a traditional educational and vocational path. To this day, songs and poems have yet to bring me fortune or fame, but I was nevertheless permanently influenced during that decadent period of my life to be true to myself in my efforts at creative expression. When writing original songs, poems, or stories, it pays handsomely (more in personal satisfaction than in cash currency) to work from a place of freedom and honesty, regardless of whether the content is popular or even believable. As Shakespeare is often quoted, "To thine own self be true." I guess this applies even when writing fiction.

As an adult, I have been writing in journals since 1978 and have filled boxes with notebooks that may be interesting for someone to read one day. I write more for the process than the product (although putting some of these thoughts into a book has been very satisfying for me). Each morning I pen a couple of pages as a form of prayer and meditation and an act of documenting my life. I enjoy the way my felt marker glides across the paper, revealing words and ideas to which I have not yet given conscious thought. I write to remember where I've been and to learn about where it is I want to go. Writing is an opportunity to see on paper what it is my heart prays in both my daydreaming and night-sleeping hours. The Spirit intercedes for me with unintelligible groans as I labor to deliver a prophecy to myself, and any who would read me, one sentence at a time. Much like in my process of painting a picture, I do not have a preconceived idea of where I am going. There is an art to unleashing the thoughts and feelings without censorship.

As in grade school, I do not often pause to consider whether what I write is fact, fiction, or a figment of my imagination. But I do know that the fruit of creative writing has become a significant piece of my spiritual journey; and since I am constantly impacted by the righteous ramblings of ancient saints and modern sinners alike, then maybe what I write will somehow be a touch of God on the life of a fellow pilgrim or even a distracted curiosity seeker. I also know that my wife loves my current pineapple buzz cut and has suggested that this may very well be the Samsonian source of my creative writing strength. Big Chief knows.

# (2)

# TRUTH OR DARE

## LYING *to* SELF *or* LIVING *by* GRACE

I am God, who enable the humble-minded to understand more of the ways of the everlasting Truth in a single moment than ten years of study in the Schools. I teach in silence, without the clamour of controversy, without ambition for honours, without confusion of argument. . . . I alone am the Teacher of truth, the Searcher of man's heart, the Discerner of his doings, and I give to each man as I judge right.

**Thomas à Kempis, as translated by Leo Sherley-Price**
*The Inner Life*

I have had truth problems ever since I was a child. It wasn't that I didn't know the difference between right and wrong, for my parents and my village raised me well, but rather that I sometimes preferred to disengage myself from the truth when it was convenient and in my best interest to do so. For instance, when I was asked what I knew about all the cars getting flat tires from tacks on the road in front of our house, my answer was simple: "Nothing." Other queries into my behavior such as "Who's been burning gasoline in the garage?" and "Where did the cigarettes go that were in your Grandma's suitcase?" all got similar answers: "I don't know" and "Not me."

I really don't know why I was such a compulsive liar as a child and teenager, but it came quite naturally to me. As young as eight years old, I was telling neighbor kids that my dad had been a quarterback for the Dallas Cowboys. About the same age, I also claimed to have been a student of karate and thought this lie to be convincing because I was willing to throw my hand, head, or foot at any stick or board any of my friends would hold in front of me. When challenged to provide proof for any of my tales, I simply grew louder in my storytelling, hoping that volume would override truth. Later in life, as my trouble with recognizing and telling the truth deepened, and the consequences of my errors grew more severe, I came to believe what some politicians and celebrities have counted on for a long time—unless there is a photograph or tape recording capturing you in the act of the purported crime, you obviously did not commit it.

In the Sermon on the Mount, Christ refers to himself as the source of Truth in his parable about solid foundations:

> Therefore everyone who hears these words of mine and puts them into practice is like a wise man who built his house on the

rock. The rain came down, the streams rose, and the winds blew
and beat against that house; yet it did not fall because it had its
foundation on the rock. (Matthew 7:24, 25)

In this familiar passage, well remembered by my generation because of the song with hand motions, Jesus was touching on universal principles that are true whether one believes them or not. One
obvious truth is that bad foundations don't survive big storms. Most
everyone has seen television footage of West Coast hillside homes
being swept away by mudslides after days on end of torrential down-
pours. Every year, vacation houses on the East Coast are overtaken
by hurricanes, rising tides, and beach erosion. No amount of bull-
dozing or sandbagging by the Army Corps of Engineers can stop the
onslaught of nature's fury and the inevitability of dangerous weather.
And apparently, no amount of evidence or common sense can stop
modern man, with his insatiable desire for more, from rebuilding
houses on the exact spots where ones were destroyed or washed out
to sea. Like those houses, it is true that lives built on shaky philoso-
phies and selfish theologies will collapse in time under the merciless
weight of reality. The storms of life have rocked my boat and leveled
my house more than once. More out of rebellion than ignorance, I
have often chosen to go down what I mistakenly perceived as the
self-reliant path of least resistance, when in fact the easier, softer
way was one of obedience to and compliance with God's will. "My
Way," as stalwartly sung over the years by Frank Sinatra and others,
has not proven to be beneficial or satisfying to the millions who have
depended on its heartfelt, albeit hollow, strategy for living.

In reading the rest of Christ's Sermon on the Mount, I see a
concise collection of simple truths that are not hard to understand

if one is trying at all to follow his documented and prescribed "narrow path" of discipleship. This collection includes, but is not limited to, directions to 1) love, 2) give, 3) pray, 4) forgive, 5) fast, 6) listen, 7) not store up earthly treasures, 8) not worry about tomorrow, 9) not judge, 10) ask, 11) seek, and 12) knock. From where I sit, these summarize all that it means to be a follower of Christ. For those of us who need specific instructions on how to live rightly, this is the 12-step program of Christianity.

No one needs to tell any of us that it is possible to live contrary to these otherworldly principles for a lifetime, even calling yourself a Christian all the while, and get by. There are millions of people who daringly live on the minimum daily requirement of God. It is also possible, I suppose, to attempt to live the life of a Christian by obeying the ten commandments (or at least four or five of them), finding some spiritual satisfaction simply by avoiding adultery, murder, and theft. The church is filled with Christians who find living by law easier than following by faith. One reason for this is that legalism is easier to believe than the scandalous message of grace. How can God really have our best interest in mind? How can his purported gifts really be free when nothing else in life is as good a bargain?

In spite of this resistance to the notion of grace, it should be noted that there is no indication, either in Scripture or in testimony from anyone I've ever met or read about, that a solid foundation for life in the here and now or the hereafter can be built upon paths of self-achieved righteousness. There is only one Truth that leads to both the kingdom of Heaven within and the Heaven of the other world, and this comes by acceptance of the righteousness of Jesus Christ. This does not mean that one is immediately obliged to embrace the moral codes of religion, though a changed heart, given enough time, will always behave differently than it did. It is the simple acceptance of his work and gift that is the key to salvation and sanctification. Only the surrendered soul can fit through the small gate. All others who dare to choose self-sufficiency or advanced ignorance to authentic and eternal Truth will have to pass through the much wider and well-traveled portal that leads to destruction. Self-destruction. Who needs a complicated theology about Heaven and Hell to know that spiritual, emotional, and mental pain in this life are but rotten fruits of self-reliance?

I used to believe in a punishing God. Then I both feared and hated that punishing God. Now I believe in a God who is all-loving and who has preordained a path to peace, happiness, and purpose for all of his children. He allows us to accept or reject this light of love, which glows warm in the heart of every man, woman, and child, thanks to the work of Christ. God loves us enough to give us this choice. It's pretty cool if you ask me. But when we choose to deny God's ways and put our faith and resources into the pursuit of our basic instincts and selfish desires, the natural and universal result is isolation, discontentment, and eventually annihilation. People who prefer to be separated from God or who choose not to believe in the One and Only get their wish of being left alone. Forever.

Each of us is responsible for the destiny of his or her soul, though the gift of unending and unfathomable joy has been given to us through the grace of God, with no strings attached. This truth is simple, too simple for many scoffers to believe and, ironically, too hard for many believers to accept. But there are many among us who can testify to the fact that living with this truth is the easier, softer way, and is not as difficult to discern as we have been told or are prone to imagine. Self-deception, along with self-reliance, always leads to self-destruction, no matter how good we happen to be at lying to ourselves or how determined we are to avoid the truth.

# (3)

# BAPTISM
## WET HUGS
### *and* DO-OVERS

In Baptism, the false self is ritually put to death, the new self is born, and the victory over sin won by Jesus through his death and resurrection is placed at our disposal. Not our uniqueness as persons, but our sense of separation from God and from others is destroyed in the death-dealing and life-giving waters of Baptism.

**Thomas Keating**
*Open Mind, Open Heart:*
*The Contemplative Dimension of the Gospel*

G rowing up in the church, I got the impression that life is most important after you die. I picked this up from all the sermons I heard about going to Heaven and not going to "H-E-double hockey sticks." From my young perspective, this seemed to be the whole point of getting saved: getting into the good place so as to make sure you definitely didn't go to the other place—the one so bad its name was considered a Class B cuss word. It was no tough choice deciding which place I'd rather go when I died; it just was never clear how to be sure I was going to end up there.

Obviously, getting dunked in the church baptistery or the camp lake was an important part because everybody did it, and all those who watched sang songs and cried and hugged you, even when you were still dripping wet, because they were glad you were going to try to go where they were trying to go, too. And maybe, if we were lucky, we'd all get to go there together. But while baptism at an early age was definitely encouraged ("You're never too young to be saved from Hell"), it seemed acceptable to get rebaptized once you were older if it was determined by a jury of your peers that you were definitely too young to know what you were doing the first time. This was a religious do-over of sorts. And though you could expect another chorus or two of "Now I Belong to Jesus" and the offer to give wet hugs to a few people, nobody cried. This made you ask yourself if the first baptism might not have counted more, and if a second baptism, not as genuine as the first, could very well undo the effects and benefits of the original one. It created quite a dilemma in the mind of the young. If it had been up to me, I probably would have gotten baptized every year, or even several times a year, just to make sure all my sins (and my derrière) were sufficiently covered.

Even after baptism, however, assurance of salvation seemed fuzzy at best to a boy with a natural knack for sinning. No one talked much about what you were supposed to do this side of death, except that you should go to church as much as possible, give your money to God (because it's his anyway and he wants it back), and the toughest requirement of all—do not sin. Of course, if you could remember all your sins at the end of the day and specifically asked God to forgive you for each and every one, you could still go to Heaven if you died in your sleep, which you didn't know rarely happened to healthy ten-year-old boys. I think it was the whole "Now I lay me down to sleep . . . if I should die before I wake" prayer that made me want to sleep in the baptistery.

Since my father was a minister, I was a regular in church before I was born. This meant that by the time I was ten years old I had gone to church approximately 1,500 times (give or take a hundred)—if you count Sunday morning, Sunday night, Wednesday night services, and both spring and fall revivals. No wonder that by then I was willing to fake any sort of sickness imaginable to be able to stay home alone on Sunday nights to watch *The Wonderful World of Disney* or *Wild Kingdom* and eat entire bags of marshmallows and semisweet chocolate chips. For this reason, I became known among my family members as a hypochondriac, when I was really just good at being sneaky. This unfortunate reputation almost cost me my life in the sixth grade. One morning, when I couldn't get out of bed due to extreme abdominal pain, my dad decided to call my bluff and wait me out, telling me the story of "The Boy Who Cried Wolf" for the umpteenth time. (Only months before, my sister had had an appendectomy, making my attack quite untimely.) Therefore, I arrived at the hospital only minutes before my appendix burst. I'm betting you could probably die in your sleep from that.

In spite of my sick-faking prowess, I would like to think that my innate drive to play hooky from religion did not contradict my sincere belief in Jesus or mean that I didn't enjoy many aspects of church. For instance, I always loved Bible school as a child, primarily because, being the preacher's kid, I usually knew most of the answers the teacher would ask in class. It wasn't until many years later, when I was teaching the boys' Bible school class at the country church where I preached, that I realized most questions asked in Sunday school can be answered with one of four responses: 1) Love Jesus, 2) Read the Bible, 3) Be a Christian, and 4) Go to Heaven. If you could get all four answers right, everyone knew you were ready to be baptized. Later, as a young minister, I baptized anyone I could get my hands on, as if collecting notches on the handle of my gospel gun. It didn't matter to me whether their motives were right or their belief was sincere. I was trained in Bible college to get them wet (saved) first and to ask questions (about faith, repentance, confession, living life, etc.) later. Every baptism was an urgent act as no one wanted to take the chance that Jesus might return in judgment before you could get the six-year-old kid in the baptistery. Each baptism was a race against time. Who would be able to enjoy Heaven with the knowledge that little Jimmy was burning in Hell forever because he wanted to wait until his grandmother could attend his baptism? Though it sounds absurd to me now, at the time it was serious business.

While I would never advise anyone to delay or avoid the act of baptism, it is no longer an urgent topic when I find myself in conversations with people concerning the beginnings of their spiritual lives. I am bothered by the fact that most times when I hear talk of someone's baptism, I can't help but notice that it is rarely mentioned in the context of that person having a spiritual awakening or surrendering his or her life to God. In fact, the temperature of the water or the mechanics of the activity itself are more ready topics of post-baptism discussion than the condition of the heart or the process of conversion. It seems to me that saying someone "accepted the gift of Christ" would be the clearest way of explaining his or her salvation decision, which in turn led to taking the step of baptism, functioning as a means of identifying with the death and resurrection of Jesus. Dead to sin, alive in Christ. I guess it's just easier, at least in my religious tradition, to say "I got baptized" when referring to this spiritual beginning point. These days, when questioned about baptism, my first impulse is to point to the book of the Acts of the Apostles in the New Testament and ask the questioner to read, pray, and get back with me if and when he or she decides this is something that seems to be important. I have found it beneficial to help people take responsibility for their own souls. They tend to grow up better this way.

Personally, I am more interested in a daily baptism of Spirit that comes from acknowledging the almighty God as the boss of my life. Immersion in the ways of Christ, fueled by the inner power and resources that cannot be controlled or manipulated by man, is the baptismal path that has major impact on how I live life and love others. If I fall into the trap of legalism, where I do and say all the right religious things but live with a hard shell around my heart, I will prevent God from changing me from the inside out. From what I have seen, getting wet doesn't change this attitude, but sincerely seeking God's will, diving into the baptismal waters of surrender and grace, does every time. This baptism of relevance, while not as likely to garner applause or get you wet hugs, pays its dividends in lasting spiritual fruit and eternal reward that begins and continues in the holy now. No one will ever question the validity of this daily do-over, and I can promise that you won't ever have to sleep in the baptistery.

# (4)

# VULNERABILITY

## CHOIR ROBES,
## CHRISTMAS FLOATS,
## *and* UNDERWEAR

"Getting down on your knees" might signify the experience of submission, of openness, or of vulnerability. But whatever the experience—however represented, however phrased, however conceived, however "felt"—this positioning of one's whole being connects the core spiritual act of the cry for help that admits one's flawed imperfection with some sort of experience of fitting-in, of connectedness to others and to a greater whole, a higher power, a God.

**Ernest Kurtz and Katherine Ketcham**
*The Spirituality of Imperfection:
Modern Wisdom from Classic Stories*

**B**y the time I was old enough to sing in the church choir, the traditional robes worn by generations of altos and tenors, sopranos and basses had been phased out in favor of wide-collared leisure suits and bright print dresses. Unfortunately, when the robes disappeared, so did the choir processional that had served as the official beginning of each worship service. As all Episcopalians and Presbyterians, most Methodists, and some Baptists can tell you, God shows up for church when the choir enters the room. So understandably there was much concern that without the choir processional the quality of our worship might go downhill. Gone was the organ-accompanied, dirge-like march of the singers walking two-by-two with arms extended, holding music folders out in front of them like holy tablets fresh from Mount Sinai. Gone were those striking crimson gowns—the color of Christ's blood, shed for all mankind—trimmed by royal golden sashes, representative of the crown of glory that awaits the faithful saints at the end of time. Even though baptismal gowns would remain in fashion in my denomination for at least another twenty years, church never felt quite the same for me without the choir robes.

Choir was almost as big a deal in my church as the sermon itself. It was considered the warm-up act for the preacher, the deliverer of the soul-draped melody that greased the skids of the heart so that the seeds of the Word of God could get planted in the right people at the right time. From my seat on the second row, the choir also gave all us little people in the audience something interesting to look at on those sleepy Sunday mornings when activity would often grind to a praying halt. Adorned in their beautiful flowing robes, those eighteen women and two men, perched high above the raised stage and oak pulpit, shone like Olympic athletes from ancient Greece awaiting their medals at the awards ceremony. Many a Sunday, when my mind wandered and my body squirmed on the squeaky pew, I would gaze past my father—hard at work convincing us sinners to love more and sin less—and imagine the details of the lives and the undergarments of each of the choir members. As we sang the first, second, and last verses of hymns I knew by heart but never understood, I would study the singers, trying to figure out which voice was coming from what face, and who was wearing or missing what piece of clothing beneath their concealing robes. If I had been any older than eight, I might have had to confess those innocent imaginings of perfumed hosiery, overstretched elastic, and baggy boxers. In my imagination it was not a pretty sight, so I am fairly sure it didn't count as a sin.

I always thought it must have been difficult to sit in the choir loft week after week, listening to the sermon, knowing that everyone was watching to see if you were going to nod and jerk, or rip the first snort of a surprise snore. Good thing I never saw anything like that happen, as I already had plenty of trouble from laughing in church. Something about the holiness of the hushed moments made almost any comment from a mischievous friend seem wildly hilarious, dooming me to the impossible task of squelching my snickers. I can still feel the twitch of pulled rib muscles and twisted internal organs, the results of years of restrained church laughter. On one occasion, when the giggle bug got hold of my best friend and me, we couldn't have stopped laughing any more than we could have comprehended the concepts of eternity or manned space flight. The more we tried to maintain our composure—even after my dad interrupted his sermon to call me down by my first, middle, and last names—the funnier our inside joke became. That was the same day that, before I saw him coming, Dad came down out of the pulpit, lifted me up by one arm and laid three rapid-fire swats on my rear end in full view of the entire congregation. As I dangled in midair trying to block the punitive blows with my free hand, I realized in that moment that I was becoming the poster boy for preachers' kids gone bad.

Though you cannot tell from the black-and-white Polaroid picture in my mother's scrapbook, my sister and I got to wear the choir robes one year before we donated them to the local Shriners or the volunteer fire department (I can't remember which). For three years running, due primarily to the artistic touch and obsessive persistence of my father, our church had won first prize in the float competition at the annual town Christmas parade. This parade usually took place on the Friday after Thanksgiving, just like the one in New York City—except that we didn't have any inflatable cartoon characters or grown men riding on little motorbikes. In our parade seven local farmers rode on their naturally festive red and green, three-wheeled tractors, each pulling a float, with marching bands from three counties interspersed between. The weather was usually football-game crisp the night of the parade, except for the year we entered our "Happy Carolers Saved from Hell" float pulled by a brand-spanking-new, holly leaf-colored John Deere. An arctic blast visited us ahead of schedule, breaking our winning streak and reversing our religious fortunes. After all, it was a statistical reality that the winner of the Christmas float competition (always a church) typically saw an increase in attendance at their morning services sometime after the New Year, though the head count usually dropped back down to normal the week after Easter.

That night, the temperature dipped below freezing and all our moms dutifully showed up with coats, hats, scarves, and gloves just as the float was about to pull onto Main Street for the judging. That which only minutes earlier had been an immaculate display of 5,000 pieces of white tissue paper neatly tucked into chicken wire, with five rows of angels wearing snow-white choir robes and dapper red ribbons, now became an array of brown and black, leaving us looking more like a sled from the homeless shelter than an award-winning float. Not even our heavenly voices could help us win the coveted trophy that year. We had spent so much time preparing the flatbed float we had forgotten to practice our song. And while some of us remembered the words to our obscure carol, the majority of us were singing lines that sounded like "Good thing Wesley Moss looked out, his hair was so uneven." From our frozen perches, we watched in disbelief as the judges awarded the noninstrumental Church of Christ first place in the float contest for their sign-language rendition of "Silent Night, A Cappella Night." In what would be my last Christmas as an anchor member of First Christian's perennial promenade, I took comfort in knowing that beneath my corduroy coat-covered choir robe I wore nothing more than a worn set of long johns and a thin layer of holy thankfulness for the Christ child that was born to make Christmas presents and parades possible.

Like my father, I would one day find myself in the role of professional minister. And though my ministry would lack the penchant for creating Christmas floats and directing Easter cantatas, it would be earmarked by the same naked (metaphorically speaking) vulnerability I once imagined and experienced beneath those choir robes. The lengthy Bible college lectures and the endless stream of chapel sermons (not to mention mounds of assigned readings, papers, and projects) I would endure and sometimes enjoy would be necessary in order to get my degree diploma and certificate of ordination, but none of these would prove to be as effective a tool for helping others as would sharing from a vault of personal experience, strength, and hope. This authentic aspect of pastoral care may certainly have been a part of my clergy training, though I do not recall any intentional coaching in this area. It is understandable if this was not emphasized by my professors, for when the ministerial student is little more than a teenager and has not yet garnered much wisdom from either good works or bad choices, it is imperative that he or she acquire the tools of original language, systematic theology, biblical hermeneutics, church history, and public speaking if he or she is to be an effective preacher of the gospel. As a result, these were the sole contents in the bag of tricks I carried into full-time church work, and were the primary, if not exclusive, source I drew from for winning souls, changing lives, and attracting crowds to what I hoped was something in the neighborhood of the kingdom of Heaven.

For those, like me, lucky enough to survive crashes of humanity and to be given another chance in the ministerial profession, this is the point at which making grave errors and having serious lapses in judgment comes in handy. To those of us willing to accept whatever God would teach us through these difficult circumstances, out of a sea of bitter emotions including despair, bewilderment, frustration, terror, regret, despondency, and disillusionment comes an education in the school of compassion, love, forgiveness, and tolerance that cannot be taught from a book. Though we who have been given this gift would gladly have taken another route if possible, it is probable that this valuable life tutorial may have been inaccessible by any means other than the painful path of ego-deflation.

It is important to note that while a life and ministry that flows from these rivers of reality and crests on the tides of transparency may be a natural fit for one who has surrendered his sufferings to God, a regular commitment to a relationship with Christ and the continuing transformation of self and selfishness is required if this desired course is to persist. There is a daily choice to rely on God that must be made, and this decision must be rooted in a commitment to specified times and places of prayer and study. There must also be the decision, as occasions arise, to love and lead out of the healed (and still healing) places from whence humility and service are realized and released. It is easy to respond to need from a place of self-knowledge and rote learning, but if we listen carefully, we can hear the Spirit knocking within our hearts, urging us to let God love others through our wounds and scars, both past and present. Admittedly, this takes courage, and requires paying attention to the ways of God. We must be ready and willing to go naked beneath the choir robe, metaphorically speaking, even when the wintry climate of our religious environs would advise us to do otherwise. This, in addition to learning to laugh in church, is an indispensable ingredient for enjoying and sharing the God journey with others.

# (5)

# GIVING

## OFFERING
## ENVELOPES
## *and*
## MAGI BUDDHISTS

From their pews below rose the ushers and elders—everybody's father and grandfather, from Mellon Bank & Trust et cetera—in tailcoats. They worked the crowd smoothly, as always. When they collected money, I noted, they were especially serene. Collecting money was, after all, what they did during the week; they were used to it. Down each pew an usher thrust a long-handled velvet butterfly net, into the invisible interior of which we each inserted a bare hand to release a crushed, warm dollar bill we'd stored in a white glove's palm.

**Annie Dillard**
*An American Childhood*

As a child, there was something about being alone in the church building, with all its dark corners and dank smells, that made me feel mischievous. I often wondered if the devil didn't hide out there during the week. Each Sunday school classroom in the basement of First Christian was used by a different age group, and I could never resist rooting through the variety of booty each contained. I was quite good at sifting through other people's stuff; I had gained much of my experience at summer church camp. As son of the camp dean and, at eight years old, much younger than the other campers, I was not obligated to show up for the classes on Old Testament dress codes or the emotional "Sword of the Spirit" competitions. I was more inclined to spend my time killing frogs and rifling through campers' suitcases. There, I would discover a gold mine of candy bars, smoke bombs, and squirt guns—all illegal, so it was not likely they would be reported as stolen if one or more of them happened to turn up missing.

It was a bit harder to snitch stuff from the Lamentators', the Odd Couples', or the Delighted Divorcees' Sunday school rooms. The adults were meticulous with their things; all their cookie packs and sugar cubes were kept in neat rows and counted each week. In addition, their big brown offering envelopes were usually empty. However, the rooms of Noah's Daughters, The Boys of Babel, and The Critters of Eden—children's classes all taught by stressed-out mothers like my mom—were a different story. There were opened boxes of vanilla wafers and stale club crackers to be scarfed, and offering baskets left with a smattering of quarters and dimes to be added to the next week's take, so the deacons' wouldn't mind counting it. These classes unknowingly kept me stocked with Baby Ruths and Grape Crush for years.

The Sunday morning offering time was always a breath of fresh air after the heaviness of the sermon and communion. As the plates were passed, the organist would start into her "all give" skating rink music and for the first time in over an hour, it was permissible to talk in church. Just before the prayers to bless the gift and the giver and the pleas for God to multiply the harvest, because God needed more money for a variety of reasons, the deacons would pass the offering plates down the line to each other with a lilt in their step as if part of a pregame warm-up for a sporting event. Though their moves were subtle, if you watched closely you might see some of the deacons patting each other on the butt in an athletic bonding ritual. You almost expected one of them to turn and spit a stream of tobacco juice in the floral arrangement and adjust his crotch before tossing the plate down the pew. This was one of many fraternal activities that, at least in our church, only men were allowed to do. And this was so because we were told it was in the Bible, though no one ever knew where to find it.

One of my many jobs as the preacher's son was to keep the pew backs stocked with plenty of sharpened golf pencils, attendance cards, and personal offering envelopes. These envelopes were for those who took seriously Jesus' admonition to not let the right hand know what the wallet was doing. (I doubted that it was the big givers who needed the anonymity provided by offering envelopes.) The slots needed replenished quite frequently, not so much because the envelopes were used for money but because they were scribbled on and filled with a. b. c. (already been chewed) gum. I learned a lot in my growing up years from reading the notes on offering envelopes that people passed to one another in church—some of it, pretty racy stuff. When it came time for my dad to give me "the birds and the bees" talk, sometime around fourth grade, he was quite surprised to learn that I had already picked up the basics, including some visual aids, from reading offering envelopes.

My take on giving money to God these days is a work in progress. While I believe the biblical tithe (10 percent) I was taught to give as a child is still a good place to start, even though it is an Old Covenant principle, I am not sure that the local church should be given complete responsibility for distributing all our monetary gifts. Don't get me wrong, I do understand the need to be financially faithful through my congregation. After all, I wouldn't want all those offering envelopes to go to waste. It's just that my ideas have shifted a bit about how the kingdom of God and money works. I now think that it is ultimately my duty to see that my dollars are given where they can best support authentic kingdom stuff. Though my wife and I live on a moderate income (by U.S. standards), we are nevertheless wealthy (by third world standards) and have come to believe that what we have is all God's and 100 percent of it is to be used to help others. My wife, Lynn, believes that when someone asks us for something, we have been instructed by Jesus to give him or her more than what he or she is asking. She gets this from the words of Jesus: "And if someone wants to sue you and take your tunic, let him have your cloak as well. . . . Give to the one who asks you, and do not turn away from the one who wants to borrow from you" (Matthew 5:40-42). So, from time to time, when we see Christ posing as the bum on the street and asking for spare change ("Hey, can I borrow a quarter?"), we try to give him or her a five- or ten-dollar bill, doing our best not to make a spectacle of ourselves. We still tithe to the church we attend; we just don't assume the funds we put in the church offering plate will always find their way to the homeless person or the drunk we may meet on the street. And since Christ said that what we do for people like this we do for him (Matthew 25:40), sometimes I think it is good for us to give our gifts directly to Jesus.

Recently I have been meditating on the gift-giving visit of the Magi to the Bethlehem home of Jesus, Mary, and Joseph. Raised on the sciences of astronomy and most likely enlightened by Eastern faiths, these Persian sages followed a miraculous star sign from as far as a continent away to present gifts of gold, frankincense, and myrrh to the newborn king of the Jews. (Their most precious gift to the Christ child, however, was not what they carried in their camel saddlebags but their act of ignoring Herod's plea to tell him the whereabouts of Israel's king.) I have not heard this theory espoused by any Christian scholars, but it does not appear to be out of the question that these special visitors to the young Christ could have been followers of Buddha or students of Confucianism; though tradition places them geographically more likely to be Zoroastrian priests from the area now known as Iran. Whatever their faith preference, it is clear they were Gentiles. And it is very interesting to me that God would bring these wise men so far from home to present gifts to the infant king of a religion not their own. I don't think it was a coincidence that these spiritual leaders from the East came to pay homage to Christ. I believe that we are given a glimpse here into the extent of how far God's grace would one day reach through the life and work of the Christ child. Perhaps even those who do not know Christianity can come to know Christ through the simple expression of belief and by bringing their gifts in sincere worship of God, as they understand God.

In reading how the Magi were guided by the star, I realize that it was not as difficult as I had previously thought for them to find the Christ child. They were not simply led to the region, the city, or the neighborhood where Jesus was—they were led to the very door of his house. You can't get any more detailed directions than that. Likewise, it has not been too difficult for me to find the Christ child in this often-hostile world. I, too, have seen the star in the east, as well as the west, and have come to worship him whose birth was foretold. I have seen this star for many years in the lives of innumerable men and women who before my very eyes have lived out a faith that works. I have also seen this star in the patterns and events that God has used to unfold truth and mystery in my own life. There are constellations of God's guidance twinkling and falling all around us with simple directions available to any who would only take the time now and then to look up and follow.

Like the Magi, my natural response to Jesus has been to bow down and worship through the bringing of gifts, not only by participating in traditional or contemporary forms of corporate worship with others. Sometimes with a song, often with a touch or a laugh, my worship is the celebration of the gift of life. Silence is golden, so I give God time and space to speak to me in the quiet hours of morning. Prayers are like incense to the nostrils of God, so I pause during the day for moments of centering calm and ask a blessing for my fellow travelers. Talents are like spices, so I lay my paintings and my stories at his feet. Harmony and color, intention and serendipity are my creative expressions of the peace and love of God in this world. I know no better way to worship the King of Kings than to bring light and life to my brother and sister with the very gifts I have been given. By the illumination of the guiding

God star within my heart, I am granted the light to see what it is I am destined to give and to whom I should pass it each day. And by this same light and the grace of God, I am forever freed from the obsession to steal vanilla wafers from the nursery and quarters from Sunday school offering baskets.

# BASEBALL

## GOD'S
## SECOND BASEMAN

I believe in the Church of Baseball. I've tried all the major religions and most of the minor ones. I've worshipped Buddha, Allah, Brahma, Vishnu, Siva, trees, mushrooms, and Isadora Duncan. I know things. For instance, there are 108 beads in a Catholic rosary and there are 108 stitches in a baseball. When I learned that, I gave Jesus a chance.

**Ron Shelton**
*Bull Durham*

I wonder what it is that drives grown-ups to ask young children the question "What do you want to be when you grow up?" Is it that they don't remember how to ask kid questions so they naturally revert to their adult obsession with work? Don't they know that bugs, toys, Christmas, and candy are the popular topics of conversation with children? Did they know what *they* wanted to be when they were six? Whatever the reason, I can't think of a question I heard more as a child except for maybe "Where did you get that?" or "What are you talking about?" Whenever I was asked that grown-up, vocational question, usually by a cheek-pinching friend of my parents or some blue-haired lady from church, I most often responded with, "I want to be a baseball player when I grow up . . . or a preacher"—unsure of which I was better suited for, and which God would be more likely to bless. Already a people pleaser, I wanted to choose the career path that would be accepted among my parent's peers and bring me some sort of local, if not international, acclaim with mine. Shaking hands at the church door next to my father after his Sunday sermons, outfitted in my dapper blue blazer and clip-on bow tie and toting a Bible bigger than our pet poodle, it was obvious to everyone that I was destined to be a minister of the gospel. God knew, however, that I was holding out for the big leagues, waiting to see what kind of curve and change-up I might develop to accompany my fair-to-middlin' fastball. What I really wanted to do was to love God and preach the Word by playing baseball.

I officially joined my first baseball team when I was eight years old. The thing I remember most about my first of many seasons on the ball diamond is that I lied about what position I played. I told all my friends and any girl that would listen that I was a pitcher when, in fact, if I was put into the game at all it was at second base; an inferior position by little league standards, second only to right field as the place the ball was least likely to be hit. Nevertheless, it was probably where I belonged at the time. After all, I was the kid who had to be told to stand beside second base, not on it. I might have known this, but at that point in my life I had watched all of my big league ball games on the radio. So there I stood on second base, outfitted with my father's floppy softball glove, a starched, oversized jersey, and a hat held up mostly by my cab-door ears. God's second baseman, out to save the world.

At that age, as I was yet to exhibit any athletic skills, I made it a point to excel in the art of chatter; a precursor to my career as a preacher. A natural loudmouth, with the dishonorable mention of "talking in class" on every one of my report cards, the baseball diamond was the only place where my knack for chatter was considered an asset by the adults in charge. Whether on the bench or in the game, I developed a reputation for leading the team choruses of "Hey, batter, batter, peanut butter, butter . . . swing!" and "He-can't-hit, he-can't-hit, he-can't-spit!" All the while I prayed silently and earnestly to the gods of balls, bats, and bases, "Please don't let it come to me." When on the inevitable occasion that a ground ball or pop fly did come my way, I sometimes surprised myself by swallowing my tongue and making the play. Just as frequently however, I watched in embarrassment and despair as the ball rolled between my legs or dropped to the ground behind me. It was a crapshoot, as far as I could tell, and part of what made the long game somewhat interesting to an undiagnosed attention deficit disorder boy like me.

It might have been my fear of having the ball hit to me that made me want to be the guy on the mound who threw the ball at the other players. It was also likely I had been influenced by the baseball biographies I read and reread each year as part of a competitive summer reading program. Day after dog-hot day, alone in my bedroom with the fan blowing muggy air through the ground-floor window, I rode the big-league trains and buses from Cleveland to New York and from Boston to St. Louis along with world-class hurlers like Dizzy Dean, Bob Feller, and of course, The Babe. These giant pitchers lived for nothing more than heaving their heroic hardballs to the cheers of Cracker Jack crowds, striking out the side, and hitting home runs for orphan boys dying of cancer in Catholic hospitals. Though I was impressed with the big-league second basemen of my day like Rod Carew and Cookie Rojas, I never aspired to be one. As good as they were at what they did, they didn't win games from their position, and their faces didn't appear on the covers of *Sports Illustrated* or *Boy's Life* magazines. The main reason was that they weren't good-looking enough. Sure, second basemen could hit leadoff singles, run out bunts, and turn acrobatic double plays. But pitchers were the handsome heroes. They threw no-hitters and saved games and when they had finished striking out the last man of the inning, they walked back to the dugout as if it was no big deal. Everyone else ran.

Not too many years later, with Cardinal Bob Gibson and Dodger Sandy Koufax on television inspiring me from major-league diamonds far away, I found myself on the mound; slinging fastballs for my Farm Bureau team past the noses of wary batters, occasionally hitting the catcher's mitt, and, every so often, the strike zone. I was at last the feared pitcher I'd dreamed of becoming, but more because I was wild than good. To this day, I can still recall the distinct sound of a baseball thumping a whirling batter in the middle of his back—I hit more than my share of batters. In little league, boys never got mad and charged the mound; they were grateful for the chance to get on base without having to swing the bat.

I was never destined to be a baseball great. My mom says, however, that I was always the best player on my teams and that she stood up for me when any of the other parents yelled at me to "hurry up" and "throw strikes." While I do not rightly recollect my level of skill, I can remember my feelings of love and importance every time I jogged onto the field in my rubber cleats and bleached-clean uniform. Like Eric Liddell in *Chariots of Fire*, who felt God's pleasure when he ran, I felt the smile of God on my shoulders each time I heard my name called as the starting pitcher or the on-deck batter, and every time I slapped a single up the middle or slid face-first into home plate. Though I always threw as hard as I could, I didn't mind when one of my friends and opposing batters would send one of my best pitches sailing safely over the outfield fence. To the chagrin of my coaches and teammates, I would sometimes meet him as he rounded third base, give him five, and say, "Nice shot, man." It didn't matter much to me whether we won or lost a game; I never thought it was really my business to care. The outcome of games always seemed to be in the hands of a higher intelligence, a general manager of sorts who was working things out as he saw fit.

Our job, I believed, was to show up and play our hearts out, leaving on the field all the sweat and fun we could, and taking home with us in our uniforms a significant portion of the dirt. The real reward for me was never the tally in the win column but the opportunity to pitch, hit, catch, run, and, at the end of the game, to dig the ice-cold root beer out from the bottom of the coach's cooler on the tailgate of his Impala station wagon. This was the fellowship after church, the conversation in the parking lot—more real and enjoyable than the actual service could ever be. This was the sacrament of the Eucharist, a soda-pop celebration of the presence of Christ who died to make this joy possible. This was the fellowship of the saints, the congregation of the boys of summer working hard at the magical game of baseball. In moments like these, how could we not feel the love and playfulness of God? Who could think of any place they would rather be? Which one of us didn't want to be this when we grew up?

# ( 7 )

# CHURCH

## BEING *and* BECOMING,
## NOW *and*
## BEYOND *the* BLUE

When we are drowned in the overwhelming seas of the love of God, we find ourselves in a new and particular relation to a few of our fellows. The relation is so surprising and so rich that we despair of finding a word glorious enough and weighty enough to name it. The word *Fellowship* is discovered, but the word is pale and thin in comparison with the rich volume and luminous bulk and warmth of the experience which it would designate.

**Thomas R. Kelly**
*A Testament of Devotion*

I am one of millions of Americans who received the first taste of God in an old-fashioned, singing, praying, and preaching, Sunday-go-to-meeting church. The fact that I am the son of a preacher man probably had some bearing upon my experiences with godly stuff, but in retrospect, I believe I was wired from birth to want the best that Heaven had to offer. (I also seemed to be naturally curious about what the people headed for Hell were doing.) Some of my earliest memories are of standing on the church pew beside my mother, shouting at the top of my lungs, "Do Lord, oh, do Lord, oh, do remember me!" To my peer group of preschoolers, volume of voice (the louder the better) reflected the quality and sincerity of your singing. Apparently understanding the meaning of the words, however, was not a priority, for my favorite chorus was primarily a plea for God to remember me when I would one day be "way beyond the blue." This I sang in spite of the fact that I also uttered, "I've got a home in glory land that outshines the sun" because "I took Jesus as my Savior, you take him too." So much for the doctrine of eternal security.

While it is possible that I was partially motivated to follow the Christian path by a guilt-fired fear of burning forever, I was nonetheless interested in doing God's will and in his feeling good about me. Being good for goodness' sake worked well for most of my childhood until I saw a girl in a tube top dancing before the Lord at a teen conference. At that point my new motivation for being a good Christian boy became wooing girls with my goody two-shoes. This lasted for one summer until I noticed that the bad boys (guys who smoked, cussed, and wore dirty jean jackets) seemed to get more attention from both good and bad girls than well-behaved, clean-cut boys like me ever dreamed of getting. So I, like many righteous males and famous preachers over the years, traded in my goodness for badness in order to get girls. My problem was that I, unlike the professional hypocrites, never figured out how to be iniquitous and maintain a righteous front while at church. During my seasons of bad behavior I would avoid the church scene altogether in order to do the immoral thing full throttle. As all social degenerates know, steering clear of uptight saints and Holy Rollers keeps the conscience from feeling any additional guilt or fresh remorse through reminders of what is right and who is wrong. This is one reason most perpetual sinners don't attend church very often. Another is they don't like being asked to sing songs they don't understand or half believe.

So in time I also became one of the millions of people who, after having heard the truth and finding it too hard to live up to, made a conscious decision to ignore it in order to explore what other appealing theories about truth might be out there. My decision included rejecting all religious teaching and information about drugs, alcohol, sex, money, and career choices. Therefore, by the age of sixteen, like many of my 1970s generation, I had become a sexually active agnostic alcoholic with a brain full of Bible and a belly full of booze. This planted me firmly in the camp outside the church and nowhere near the kingdom of God. According to what I would later learn in Bible college, the fact that I had once known the truth and had repeatedly turned my back on it qualified me for what is referred to in Matthew 12:31 and Hebrews 6 as "blaspheming against the Holy Spirit"— interpreted by some to be the unforgivable sin. Fortunately for me, the God I understand doesn't feel that way, for I have received more than my share of last chances in spite of a history of backsliding. As a result of this bottomless well of Christ's bountiful grace, I have found my way back inside the walls and the ways of the church and enjoy unlimited opportunities to share my story of redemption with those in need of hope, direction, and unconditional love.

While there are countless directives in the Old and New Testaments for living the righteous life, I have gleaned three principles from Scripture-tested living that I think contain the nuts and bolts to living in the sacred now. From these sources, confirmed by my own experience and that of mature disciples I have studied over the years (such as the Thomas's: Thomas Merton, Thomas Kelly, Thomas Keating, and Thomas Moore), I rest secure in the knowledge that, when in full compliance with the following values, I am a progressing pilgrim journeying with complete confidence that the kingdom of Heaven is within me.

## Value 1: Make and maintain a personal connection with God

I am responsible for my relationship with the Creator. I come into this world alone and leave in the same company. Connecting with God is, first of all, an individual and private matter, though it rarely remains an activity of isolation. God makes this connection possible as I partner with him for the willingness to do the work. For me this means a nonnegotiable daily practice of surrender, seeking the mind and spirit of Christ with holy readings, journaling, and prayers. It also includes being true to the desires God plants in my heart to create, embrace, celebrate, and strive, making a point to listen to his voice through his Spirit and agents in this world. As the rapid currents of selfish ambition would sweep me into a desperate search for financial security and ego satisfaction, the best assurance I have of staying close to God's will and steering clear of the influence and love of mammon is the regular exercise of asking God to keep me in his way, and trusting in his ability to do just that.

Brother Lawrence writes of practicing the presence of God in all of life, making even our daily work an act of loving God. And while we may pursue God by being attentive to his will for us as we work, play, create, and rest, seeking God must be intentional to be productive. My wayward heart does not naturally crave the pure things of God, but longs for the empty canyons of fleshly satisfaction and self-centered delusion. This is but one reason why I need more than what comes naturally to me; I must have direct access to the supernatural. In the book *Alcoholics Anonymous*, Bill Wilson, referring to his and others' miraculous relief from alcoholism, wrote "that God could and would if he were sought." If this is true, as millions of recovering alcoholics can attest, then it is also possible that God can't and won't if he is not. God makes this choice possible through the double-edged sword of free will. The surrender of this free will to the will of God is the gateway to eternal life that is more about a quality of existence in the holy present than a quantity of pie in the sky by and by.

## Value 2: Experience the journey in the company of others

In spite of my lifelong desire to be a James Dean-type rugged individualist, in some way or another it has become an imperative reality that I trek the path of spiritual growth in the company of other travelers of like mind and soul. This means gathering frequently with those who would call themselves Christ-followers. This also includes not shying away from those who seek God but do not necessarily pledge allegiance to the Christian flag. These days I am not so quick to label people as unsaved, heathen, or lost. When applied too casually, tags such as these help create an atmosphere of separation between "us" and "them" that can inhibit or prohibit relationships with the very people with whom we would share our faith. Sometimes, God even uses people who would not consider themselves believers to minister to us. On numerous occasions I have gathered with people with whom I shared a creative but not spiritual common bond that, unbeknownst to them, encouraged me in my God walk. Go figure.

My perspective on the church is that her members consist of believers, inside and outside the walls of a particular congregation who may or may not practice well the faith they espouse. It is by the work of Christ that the grace of God saves us, not by any level of obedience we exhibit. It appears to me that the church, rather than being an exclusive religious order, may well be inclusive of many God-followers outside of our traditional parameters of Christianity. It may be that many in our midst who seek to follow the light of reason, inner truth, or higher consciousness as best as they know how have yet to recognize that this is the light of Christ at work in them.

This perspective, one that encourages me to look down a progressive timeline at the development of faith, solves many dilemmas regarding various spiritual practices. It also allows people who may not know they are being saved, but who nevertheless nurture a mustard seed of faith in their hearts, to be my (actual, if only potential) brothers and sisters in Christ. This is the true work of evangelism: seeing people with a God's-eye view and loving them for who they are as well as who they are becoming.

## Value 3: Practice Christ's love through service and sacrifice

As has always been the case, there is much talk of evangelism in church leadership circles. The business-like air surrounding some conversations about reaching the lost is often confusing and bothersome to me. Attendance figures are thrown around as if they are more important than the people they represent. To be blunt, when

I hear impassioned speeches for the need to "win souls" I can't help but feel that I am in a multi-level marketing seminar being pumped up to earn diamond pins or a pink Cadillac. While I don't doubt that there is value and validity in "leading people to Christ," and that Jesus is definitely interested in all souls coming to know him, Scripture tells me that Christ is the one who "came to seek and to save what was lost" and that when he is lifted up he would "draw all men" to himself. In Acts 2:47 Luke records, "And the Lord added to their number daily those who were being saved." The *Lord* added, not the miraculously multilingual, blue-collar disciples turned articulate apostles.

The Holy Spirit works by making the stuff of Heaven—not on eBay or the Home Shopping Network—available to a hungry world in search of a solution to emptiness and despair. And the vehicle of choice appears to be one fragile and frail church attempting to live out the principles of the kingdom of God while juggling career, family, houses, and bowling schedules. By stepping up to ask my friend or neighbor, "What can I do to help you?" or humbly praying, "Here I am Lord. Send me," and then actually going, I fulfill my destiny of faith and complete the cycle of rebirth by dying to self. This is the church in action, fueled by the love of God for the benefit of those who are lost and in need of relational redemption.

From the letter of James, the true religion that God considers pure and faultless is "to look after orphans and widows in their distress and to keep oneself from being polluted by the world." From what I have seen, the former helps make the latter possible. There is nothing like service with a smile and a sacrificial spirit to help relieve one from the bondage of self and the merciless obsession for more of everything. Nothing takes my mind off of me like serving those who have nothing to give in return or loving those who can give me nothing but reasons not to love them. Christ's mandates for the church to love, pray, give, forgive, comfort, encourage, share faith, and make disciples are as much for our own health and well-being as for the expansion of his kingdom. As they say in 12-step rooms all over the world, "You gotta give it away in order to keep it." This is true today and will likely still be true "way beyond the blue."

# (8)

# MIRACLES

## FLEABITES *and* LIGHTNING STRIKES

In the very first days of the order, when Saint Francis was together with some of his companions in order to speak of Christ, he ordered one of the brethren to speak of God as the spirit led him to speak . . . That all spoke with the inspiration of the Spirit was soon underscored by a clear sign. For in the midst of them appeared the Blessed Christ in the form of a beautiful young man. He blessed them with such a sense of ineffable sweetness that they were rapt outside of themselves and acted as dead men, so oblivious were they of the world around them.

**Lawrence Cunningham**
*Brother Francis: An Anthology of Writings by and About St. Francis of Assisi*

L ike most miracles, I never saw it coming. The real miracle was that I survived to tell about it. One summer in the late 1960s, my dad took one of my best friends and me to a Christian camp for college students in the Kiamichi Mountains of Oklahoma. My friend Phil Long and I had likely been brought along so that Dad could go do what he loved best without getting too much grief. Next to going to school to either teach or get another degree, religious camps and conferences were the things my dad got excited about. And while he may have been hoping that my friend and I would catch on to some of the hippied-up Jesus stuff being preached under the big tent every night, I think he went mainly because he loved God and wanted God to be happy with him. I hadn't learned enough yet to know that God wasn't happy with me, but I remember being curious as to what God might do for me if I memorized the names of the books of the Bible and prayed for a miracle. I had heard if you had faith and prayed hard enough you could get one, but I wasn't sure I would know it if I saw one. In spite of my lack of faith and short prayers, I was about to witness my first miracle.

This being a camp for adults, most of the sessions were lectures and sermons which my friend and I found to be boring; except for the one about Ouija boards and demon possession, which spooked me out and made me want one of those boards for Christmas. My dad must have missed that session because Santa Claus brought me a Ouija board that year. (If anyone reading this still thinks that this "game" is a harmless means of entertainment, think again. The Ouija board is nothing less than a portal into a dark and scary underworld. I kid you not! Beware!) Anyway, since Phil and I were kind of young, about ten I think, we skipped as many of the lectures as we could and, along with another kid named Jay, found a wide range of diversions to occupy our restless little minds and bodies. I remember us finding a pack of donkeys that wandered along a well-beaten trail on the other side of the camp fence. We were delighted to discover that they didn't seem to mind if we rode them as they wound their way through the woods on a path they had probably walked their whole lives. This was a lot of fun until we reluctantly admitted to each other that we had developed an intense itching in our crotches, which turned out to be fleabites. Surviving that wasn't my first miracle, but it did lead to my attending the sermon sessions so that I could ask God to heal me of the itching and, if it was his will, to get me a Ouija board.

One particularly hot day that week, a thunderstorm rolled into the mountains, dumped buckets of rain on the camp, and brought a welcome coolness to the air and scorched earth. People had been praying for rain all week, as there were forest fires in the vicinity that had the potential to threaten the campground if not brought under control. The word *miracle* was on the lips of many who believed God had personally saved us from destruction by fire with our own little rain shower. I remember running under a huge oak tree for cover from the sudden deluge that had caught me by surprise, ignoring the age-old warnings about standing under trees during lightning storms. In the next instant, I was blinded by a flash of light and knocked to the ground by a deafening boom that exploded over my head. I heard a cracking noise that seemed to run the length of the big tree and up my spine, and I was overcome by the smell of ozone and seared oak. I must have sprung to safety like a startled rabbit for the next thing I knew I was under a shelter more than a hundred feet away looking back in amazement at the smoking tree.

As my hearing slowly returned, I became aware of a loud and steady drumming and I realized that I was under the big tent surrounded by what appeared to be a thousand hands in the air. A crowd of voices chanted and sang, "Jesus!" (drum, drum, drum) "Jesus!" (drum, drum, drum). Tambourines rattled and feet stomped to the droning revival beat. Some guy beside me was shouting "Hallelujah! It's a miracle!" I thought at first that he had seen me just miss getting killed by lightning. Then I wondered if he somehow knew that my private itching was beginning to wane—another miracle. However, he was referring to the much-needed rain.

This, my first experience with a miracle, assuming at least one of the events was miraculous, was also my first exposure to the natural skepticism that people have toward Heaven-sent intervention. I overheard some people saying that day that the rainstorm was not a miracle, only nature doing its thing. Someone else said, "The age of miracles has passed. The Bible is clear on this." All I knew was that God seemed very real to me in that moment and that the coed in front of me with the halter top and cutoffs looked profoundly beautiful. Since I was nine or ten years old and still unaware of the opposite sex, the fact that I noticed her and didn't want to give myself a cootie shot was yet another miracle.

Years later as a student at Cincinnati Bible College, I remember reading that in the months following the Cane Ridge (Kentucky) revival and other such nineteenth-century outpourings of the Holy Spirit—along with all their supernatural phenomena and emotional outbursts—there was an unexplainable spike in pregnancies. Apparently spirituality and sexuality have been kissing cousins for quite some time. Without getting off too far on this tangent, I think it is safe to say that God stuff can be volatile, if not downright sexy, and should be handled with the care that it deserves. Just ask the thousands of professional pastors who have left their ministries, never to be heard from again, due to extramarital affairs, a serious vocational hazard. I guess anytime a man of God doesn't leave his wife for another woman (or man) could also be considered a miracle.

In my twenty-plus adult years of striving for spiritual growth, I have come to believe in miracles again. I have seen the marvel of recovery and restoration in my life and in thousands of alcoholics just like me. I have seen the scriptural and 12-step principles of "trust God," "clean house," and "help others" transform me from the inside out when my own shallow prayers and self-determination proved ineffective. I have come to recognize the miraculous hand of God in all that grows and glows in nature and in the seasonal cycles that bring death and rebirth into our lives each year. I think the way my cats communicate and exhibit affection, the changing colors of the western sky at twilight, and the taste of a zucchini freshly plucked from a backyard garden are all out-of-this-world experiences. Who can inhale and savor the sweetness of a perfectly formed American Beauty rose, listen to the chorus of frogs and crickets after a summer shower, and feel the warm healing power of a loving hug without realizing that God is so much more than we are capable of conceiving? Personally, I see no harm in labeling as miraculous the daily signs and wonders that happen outside the realm of human influence. I say if God is behind it, it must be a miracle. Most miracles I never see coming, though they drive through my neighborhood every day. However, if I am tuned in and on the lookout for the hand of God, I will see miracles at every turn, in every person I meet, and in every breath I take. The greatest miracle of all I suppose is the grace that allows us to open our eyes, ears, and hearts to experience the touch of God in every corner of our lives, and survive ourselves to tell others about it.

# (9)

# WORSHIP

## OUTDOOR SANCTUARIES
### *and the*
## ANIMAL KINGDOM
### *of* GOD

Particular places, like particular times, lose any ultimate significance when "prayer without ceasing" is realized—when God's Presence is seen without boundaries. . . . Many of us head for mountain tops or waterfronts. There is a particular spaciousness in those places that encourages us to see farther than elsewhere. A perspective seeps in that awakens our sense of simple belonging in this flow of nature which bears and consumes our bodies. We become more porous to that usually dammed up spring of Living Water deep within us—that fresh stream washing clean the lens of our perception and revealing an unspeakable Presence.

**Tilden Edwards**
*Living Simply Through the Day:*
*Spiritual Survival in a Complex Age*

The small rental cottage I shared with my wife and two cats was about as close to highway NC-12 as any house on Hatteras Island. However, as I left my front door and turned east, a short three-block walk would lead me to the shores of the ever-changing Atlantic Ocean with its daily variations on the colors green and blue: turquoise and indigo, emerald and cerulean, viridian and ultramarine. One block in the other direction lay the calm, yet volatile, Pamlico Sound with its burgeoning population of birds, insects, reptiles, and fish. The driveway in front of our place was a narrow sandy lane bordered on both sides by pines, cedars, scrub oaks, and various vegetations native to eastern North Carolina. Walking out my door, I was showered by the mingling fragrances of salty sea grass and sweet honeysuckle blossoms that had bloomed at full volume in the previous week. An alluring blend of scents, this combination stirred my imagination and sense of wonder much like the English boxwoods and climbing ivy of my grandmother's Virginia backyard did for me as a child. My first impulse was to stop in my tracks, lift my nose to the sky, breathe deeply the smells of earth and heaven, and utter the prayer "Thank you, God." As if in response, the songs of the cardinal and the mockingbird singing "Life is beautiful" and "All is as it should be" called down from the trees and telephone wires. Within a hundred yards of my home, I was energized by the touches of God; my heart was directed in worship by the goodness and glory of his creation. The great outdoors is the cathedral where I most easily worship the divine Spirit. I know that God lives everywhere, but it seems to me that when push comes to shove, he prefers to hang outside.

Having grown up in the home of a preacher and later becoming a minister myself, I can safely say that I have spent half of my life in a church building. It was there that I was taught, or caught, that the principal place where God worship took place was in the sanctuary services where singing, praying, preaching, the sacramental observances of baptism and communion, and the collection of tithes and offerings formally ushered us into the presence of the Almighty. I was told that we dressed up on Sundays to present our best to God, which led me to believe that God was very concerned with outward appearances. It was often said that we should be quiet and reverent in the house of the Lord, which taught me that God was not much fun and lived in a stuffy building that was empty most of the time. The God I was taught about must have been very lonely. Only a few people were ever allowed to speak publicly in church—mostly men in suits with tight collars and red faces, leaving me with the impression that God wasn't all that interested in what kids or women had to say. From these experiences with worship, I concluded that Heaven, the place where saints and angels would worship around the throne of God for eternity, was going to be a very dull place.

Though I didn't identify it as worship at the time, I had much more interesting and far more interactive devotional experiences as a child while playing outside. For instance, I never felt as close to God as when sailing my Western Flyer bicycle home from school on a Friday afternoon in May or soaring face-first down a snow-packed hill on my Flexible Flyer sled in December. (Things with the word *fly* in them were very big sellers in the '60s and the concepts of flying and worshipping God often went hand in hand for me.) Likewise, nothing compared to the spiritual bliss I felt on the kickball diamond as I booted a home run over the heads of my elementary classmates or flew my kite at the reservoir on an autumn afternoon. I had no better offering for God than the trumpet solo I played for "I'd Like to Teach the World to Sing" (made famous by the "It's the Real

Thing" Coca-Cola commercial) during a junior high band concert or when I strummed my guitar and sang "Pass It On" around the fire at church camp.

Could anything have conjured up pleasant thoughts of God more than listening to choruses of chirping crickets from a dew-soaked pup tent or taking a cool skinny-dip on a warm summer's night? Wasn't my heart opened wide to the wonders of God's miraculous reach when I was lying on my back watching stars blink and fall, and when I was following the rising yellow-orange moon from my open bedroom window while filling the sill with sunflower seed shells? My lust for life was insatiable and my search for beauty inexhaustible. This is how it was for me for years; I don't think I knew any better. Perhaps it takes a childlike mind and character to worship God in the everyday, everyway world like that. Perhaps this is what Christ meant when he said, "Unless you become like little children, you will not be able to see God's kingdom" (Matthew 18:2, 3, paraphrased). If this is the case and cause for true God worship, it is my goal never to grow too old in spirit to miss the wonder of touching God's face with the mind and perspective of a spiritual child.

While we were still newlyweds, my wife, Lynn, and I made a decision to sell everything we owned and travel around the country in a recreational vehicle. (Go ahead. Let me hear you say "That there, Clark, is an RV.") Since we didn't own much to sell, we couldn't afford much of a camper, but the 1977 Dodge I bought and cleaned up served us well in spite of the fact that it had been ridden hard and put away wet. Lynn and I had concluded that since we didn't have any debt or children, we should do whatever we wanted while we were still young, and we both had a lot of places we had never been. So over the next three years, we crisscrossed the country and Canada a total of ten times, touching as many states as we could, financing the journey by me singing God songs and Lynn selling my CDs and her handmade beaded jewelry at churches. We never made a lot of money, but we got by and lived well, for a couple of gypsies.

Acting like retirees, we dawdled and rambled at our own pace, never in a hurry to get anywhere. Along the way, we spent days and even weeks at a time at state and national parks, hiking, painting, reading, napping, and soaking in the life and culture unique to each place. In the winter, we could be found in the deserts of New Mexico and Arizona, or on the southern beaches of Florida or California. In the springtime, we wandered across the Rocky Mountains of Colorado and Montana or made a beeline back east to visit our families in Virginia and Georgia. Come summer we drove north and headed west across Highway 2, the northernmost east-west route across America; taking in the Great Lakes from the coasts of Michigan and Wisconsin, exploring small towns, and visiting Native American monuments and reservations in the Dakotas. (Travel hint: If ever in the Black Hills of South Dakota, skip Mount Rushmore and visit the much more spectacular Crazy Horse Memorial.) Late August was the perfect time to saunter about the Pacific Northwest, basking in the moss-laden forests and wild, rocky coastlines of Washington and Oregon. But by harvest time, we inevitably found ourselves back in the Midwest— leading retreats and camping out at the Horse Park in Lexington, Kentucky, and tasting the quiet and simple life of the Amish country in northern Ohio. It may come as a surprise for you to hear me say this, but after seeing most of the majestic wonder of the American West, I must tell you that, for my money, there is no place more beautiful in autumn than Brown County State Park or Hoosier National Forest in south-central Indiana. John Cougar Mellencamp can attest to the fact that God indeed lives in Indiana, at least during the fall and basketball season.

During one of our coast-to-coast treks, we decided to take a swing through Alberta, Canada, and catch the Calgary Stampede, the self-proclaimed world's largest rodeo. While camping at a mom-and-pop RV park outside the city, we discovered much to our delight that we were the guests of an active gopher colony. As my wife, our cats, and I are huge fans of the American prairie dog, we fell in love with these friendly rodents incapable of harming anyone but cattle ranchers and rodeo queens. As we learned, ranchers aren't fond of gophers or prairie dogs because they say horses can step in their holes and break a leg (although I've yet to hear of this actually happening). Rodeo queens don't like them either because they can step in the holes when practicing their stroll to the stampede stage in their backyards, which makes them look bad when they fall down. I heard of one rodeo princess so committed to following in her queen's footsteps that when the queen stepped in a gopher hole en route to the crowning stage, the princess stumbled in and out of the same hole as if on cue. Needless to say, when we found out that God's gophers near our campsite were being systematically poisoned by the innocent-looking Mom and Pop, we were noticeably upset, particularly since there didn't seem to be any cattle ranchers or rodeo queens in the vicinity. Reluctantly ruling out eco-sabotage, my wife and I revisited for a day the idea of becoming vegetarians to protest the mistreatment of all animals everywhere, as we believe that animals teach us much about love and the character of God. But since we couldn't remember the last time we had eaten any gopher or horsemeat, we decided to ponder other options.

The Calgary Stampede was, pound for pound, the most competitive rodeo I've ever witnessed in my suburban cowboy life. And I've been taking in the sights and smells of ridin' and ropin' stockyard animals since I was eight years old. I will never forget my first rodeo in Salina, Kansas. In 1968 when Robert Conrad of *Wild, Wild West* fame came galloping out atop his royal palomino, sporting a cobalt sequined jacket that glistened in the spotlight like diamonds in a Tiffany's showcase, I'd never seen anything more blue or more beautiful. I'm not sure if it actually happened or not, but I have a faint memory of Mr. Conrad (aka James West) reaching down and swooping me up out of the stands and onto the saddle of his steed to circle the arena and wave to our cheering fans. Wow, what a night!

At the stampede, I was most impressed with the precision, the uniforms, and the pace of Her Majesty's Royal Canadian Mounties. An anomaly at the rodeo to be sure, the Mounties seemed like a throwback to a simpler time when saving the day and enjoying the ride were higher-held values than straining to earn more money and gain more acclaim at every outing. While most of the crazed bull-riding and beer-drinking fans slept or used the porta-potties during the red coats routine, I was hypnotized by the lo-fi, slow-motion show. Being as it was in the middle of an arena where every other event was loud, fast, and continuously selling something, it reminded me of the kind of countercultural experience that I envision the church could demonstrate if we paid more attention to how we live, serve, and worship.

Most American churches I have visited in recent years tend to worship like they drive: on a mission from God, anxious to get where they're going. Though I know we all battle to overcome it, there is a gravity toward consumerism that affects our church style, pace, and programming; it's difficult to catch our breath or get ten seconds in a worship experience for reflection or meditation. Loud, fast, and continuous don't serve us well when the purpose of our gathering is to experience the Mighty One in authentic and meaningful moments of spirit and truth. To avoid being accused of being critical without offering a real solution, I would like to propose that we consider hiring the Royal Canadian Mounties to train our ushers and worship leaders, and then meet outside as often as possible surrounded by birds, gophers, and groundhogs. The deacons could pass the baskets on bicycles while the musicians fly kites from their instruments. We'd have to remember, however, to warn the preacher about the gopher holes. We wouldn't want him to fall in one and break a leg or worse yet, become a vegetarian.

# ( 10 )

# HAPPINESS

## BICYCLES
### *and*
## ICE CREAM

Happiness is not what happens when everything goes the way you think it should go; happiness is what happens when you decide to be happy.

**Marianne Williamson**
*Everyday Grace: Having Hope, Finding Forgiveness,*
*and Making Miracles*

Ever since my celebrated liberation from training wheels, around age four or five, I have had an ongoing love affair with my bicycle. Sometime around 1964, when the Beatles were first flying to the shores of America, I was flying on a little red two-wheeler, my heart racing with excitement as I illicitly darted down the streets and alleys of my Williamsburg, Virginia home. Streets were supposedly off limits to bicycling kids my age, but everyone knew that sidewalks were for girls and old people. Besides, the curb at each corner was a real momentum buster that could keep a world-class speedster like me from achieving his full potential. Unbeknownst to my parents, I also followed the older, though not smarter, kids as they trailed the summer mosquito truck spraying its thick cloud of toxic fumes in which we could make believe we were airborne. This was as close as we could get to being Green Lantern or Superman, using our superpowers to disappear and to breathe noxious gases and not die. (The jury is still out on what sort of brain damage we might have incurred on these daredevil rides, but I haven't had a mosquito within a mile of me in years.) Other times I took advantage of my Aquamanesque heightened sense of hearing that alerted me to the presence of an ice cream man in distress three blocks away, with too many treats on his hands. Up, up, and away I took off on my bicycle to save the day, consuming a dripping orange-and-vanilla pushup; then rushing home in time to alert my mom of his arrival, acting as if I hadn't seen my favorite snack vendor in years. Bicycles and ice cream always made me happy.

By the time I was ten years old I had discovered that my bicycle was more than just a vehicle for having fun; it was a way of life, a source of livelihood (if you had a paper route), and an icon of a subculture not unlike that of the motorcycle. The only difference in our view was that we weren't required to wear black leather to ride.

And, though we didn't have the accessories to choose from that are available to today's fashionable biking enthusiast, banana seats and sissy bars were standard equipment. In addition, every block had one spoiled kid lucky enough to sport the much-coveted Vroom! Vroom! Having one of these high-tech, battery-operated instruments of noise automatically entitled the owner to be outright leader of the two-wheeling pack on the block, whether or not he exhibited any leadership qualities. The rest of us used clothespins and playing cards, which we thought sounded more authentic anyway.

To anyone still enjoying his or her childhood, riding a bike, as with its motorized two-wheeled counterpart, has always been a passport to cultural freedom, as well as a vehicle for societal rebellion. Upon saddling up a bike, the rider is instantly freed from the constraints of parental authority and unleashed to ride like the wind, leaving in a cloud of dust all orders to clean up, pick up, or take out anything. On your bicycle you can pop wheelies, ride with no hands, even race in front of cars if you are so inclined.

The long-gone kids on my childhood street rode bikes as if they were charting new territory or practicing a new religion. Flooded with fervor and abandon, we all carried scabs and scars as proof of our devotion. One time I was riding alone on the shoulder of a busy four-lane when a late-merging car sideswiped me, leaving me with a 4-inch gash on my left calf. To avoid certain death or worse, a destroyed bicycle, I held onto the rear door handle of the car until the lady passenger could persuade her husband driver to stop and check on me. Convinced my parents would punish me for riding on the highway, I hid my wound, which probably could have used a tetanus shot and a dozen stitches. This little secret forced me to miss out on much respect and many brownie points I might have earned had I been able to show my badge of honor to my biking peers. This sacrifice might very well have even cost me my chance at being the first leader of the pack in my neck of the woods without a Vroom! Vroom!

Twenty years later, virtually homeless and penniless, I sat dejected and confused on the steps of the fourth drug and alcohol rehab I had patronized in as many years. Having drunk and drugged away a marriage, a career, and nearly a life by age thirty, I had wasted many opportunities to be a success story and more than a few chances at having a great comeback. What I did not know on that, both the darkest and brightest day of my life, was that I was about to finally get sober to stay—thanks to God and the spiritual program of a 12-step fellowship. New to recovery, with more time and energy on my hands than I had money, I would soon rediscover the economical value and endorphin-pumping joy of riding a bicycle. Along with my friend Chris, one of my new allies in abstinence, I rode my Raleigh hybrid bike all over Cincinnati, Ohio, finding in the face-first breezes and the carefree thoughts that accompanied them my desire to live and the will to go to any lengths to stay sober.

I have observed over the years that there are a handful of activities in which it is virtually impossible to participate and not be happy: eating ice cream is one and riding a bike is another. (If I were a psychiatrist, every time someone came to see me for depression I would prescribe eating ice cream while riding a bicycle every day for a month.) As quoted at the beginning of this chapter, Marianne Williamson confirms what I have found to be true in my life: "Happiness is not what happens when everything goes the way you think it should go; happiness is what happens when you decide to be happy." Riding my bicycle on a daily basis helped me get used to the idea of being happy again, when my preferred feelings for years prior seemed to hover somewhere between anxious and desperate. Now, I could make the decision to be happy and take certain actions to achieve this result, any time I wanted. At the time this seemed like an amazing discovery.

During those what now seem to have been magical days, many of my bicycle rides with Chris began with a midnight phone call. "Hey. What are you doin'?" "Nothing much. Watching Letterman and chain-smoking Marlboros." "Wanna travel?" "You bet. I'll meet you halfway." And off we would go into the night, the perfect time for traveling big-city streets. With not too many cars to dodge, we pedaled down the middle of the road, ran red lights, and felt as if we owned the city. We regularly buzzed through rough sections of town like Over-the-Rhine with our headlights off, passing by gangs of people huddled on street corners—too fast for anyone to touch us, though they often yelled, "Hey, give me that bicycle!" Smart enough not to comment aloud, I thought to myself, *You can't touch me. I'm the Green Lantern, invisible behind a veil of smoke and darkness.*

One year later, feeling strong enough in my reliance upon God to keep me on the path of sobriety, I packed up my bike and took it with me to Europe. My mother was living in Germany at the time, so this gave me a home base from which to travel. Using a nontopographical map, I plotted out a 300-mile, one-way trip that would bring me back to Heidelberg within two weeks. Brimming with anticipation of the freedom trek I was taking, I boarded a southbound train to France from whence I would begin my ride back to

Germany. Being somewhat young and in relatively good shape, I had not considered the terrain I would be facing; confident that, as sung in *The Sound of Music*, I would "climb every mountain." I had no way of knowing that the first leg of my trip would be up—straight up—one of the mountains in the heart of the Tour de France course. In fact, just days earlier Greg LeMond had led the famous race up that very mountain, though he had likely traveled about 30 mph faster than my pace.

Loaded with 75 pounds of pack on my back, I spent the first day of my trip switching back and forth with just enough speed to keep my bike upright, listening to Cat Stevens on my headset, and sucking down my water too fast. The burn in my leg muscles was like no pain I had ever experienced, but the intense beauty of the azure, sunlit sky was almost enough to make me ignore the hurt. I felt like Icarus, climbing closer and closer to the sun, unaware that my wax was melting and my wings were about to come off. At times, it seemed the mountain was so steep that the force of gravity might pull me backward and leave me like a turtle turned over on the road, legs wiggling and arms groping for the right angle with which to right myself. What with all the difficulty the climb presented for me, the ride down the other side made it all worthwhile. Swooping down out of the sky at 50 mph, I glided for what seemed like a lifetime past lush, green forests and through verdant valleys, winding my way down to a cozy village nestled at the bottom of the mountains. I can still recall the sweet smells of earth and air and the sight of window boxes on every house, filled with petunias and chrysanthemums, welcoming me without words to a place I would have never found without my bicycle. I also remember being happy and having an undeniable craving for ice cream.

# (11)

# COMMUNION

## BREAD CHICLETS
### *or the*
## BODY *of* CHRIST?

> My whole soul was filled with the unutterable peace of the undisturbed opportunity for communion with God—with the sense that at last I had found a place where I might, without the faintest suspicion of insincerity, join with others in simply seeking his presence. . . . and since that day . . . Friends' meetings have indeed been to me the greatest of outward helps to a fuller and fuller entrance into the spirit from which they have sprung; the place of the most soul-subduing, faith-restoring, strengthening and peaceful communion, in feeding upon the bread of life, that I have ever known.
>
> **Caroline Stephen (as selected by Jessamyn West)**
> *The Quaker Reader*

Communion, the only food associated with church outside of the covered-dish dinner, always came at the worst time on Sunday mornings for me. Having been roused out of bed at the crack of dawn and rushed through a prisoner's breakfast of cereal and toast, I was starving by 11:30, when the deacons lined up to serve the mini-sacraments. These men, usually dressed in ill-fitting suits, were farmers mostly, and I could count the shades of their red necks in contrast to the white lines left by their Dekalb Corn hats. They always had such a holy expression up there at the Jesus table, mumbling wordy prayers in voices not quite their own; but I knew they didn't act so holy on other days of the week because I often overheard other church members telling my mom and dad about the men's shortcomings and trespasses that needed to be forgiven. After much blessing of the cup and loaf with words like *hither* and *beseech*, which no one used any other time, the men took turns serving the trays of crackers and juice—with prophetic knowing carefully skipping all who had yet to be baptized. This was known as our "passover," and had its origins in ancient churchdom.

Though the communion bread chiclet was known to be a holy, nonnutritive foodstuff—not unlike the unleavened bread the Israelites baked up hard in the wilderness—I know for a fact that some people ate it as a snack to tide them over until they could get home to their pot roast. I knew one kid who took a handful every time the tray came around. I would have liked to have had seconds, but I never had the nerve to take more than one. After all, it had taken a real commitment—giving my heart to God and getting water-dunked—to be able to take the weekly chiclet in the first place. I wasn't about to lose my communion privileges by being greedy and getting caught by one of the holy, rednecked deacons.

By all admissions, though, the real treat was the mini-cup of grape juice that was served as a chaser for the bone-dry chiclet. I didn't know a kid who wouldn't have gladly whipped out a straw and sucked dry a dozen of those cups in a flash if he could've gotten away with it. Being the preacher's kid and having access to all the rooms of the church, I often found the leftover communion trays in the kitchen, inviting and unguarded. More than once, I desecrated the temple by finishing off the undrunk cups of Christ's nonalcoholic wine. I couldn't help myself and trusted his payment for my sin to cover this indiscretion.

These leftovers were often saved for the Sunday night service, which existed mainly to give people who skipped morning church the opportunity to have their supper with the Lord and not have to wait in fear and guilt until the next Sunday. Of course, if you wanted to take communion at Vespers, the Bible name for Sunday night church (so we thought), you had to walk down to the front row during the third verse of the sad hymn about Jesus having to die for our sins because we were worms. This was so that everyone would know who had something more important to do on Sunday morning than to be in the Lord's house and to share his chiclet supper.

In more recent times, life has unfolded for me the truth that the sacrament of communion, reenacting Christ's last supper with his disciples before his crucifixion and resurrection, is much more than eating and drinking prayer-blessed, sample-sizes of juice and crackers in a somber church auditorium. Communion is about regular and authentic contact with other God-believers in random as well as scheduled get-togethers. The fellowship that occurs at these gatherings is nothing less than an invitation for the God of season changes, birth, rebirth, and starry, starry nights to mix and mingle with those in search of spirit and truth. And where two or three are gathered—in bowling alleys, coffee shops, or 12-step meetings—God is there, participating at full strength through the interactions, feelings, ideas, imaginings, and muses of this chosen people. This is church in ways that some may have difficulty seeing or accepting; for this congregation does not require money, buildings, or ordained leaders to ensure its appropriateness and propriety. This church is alive and well and thrives in all continents and races. Every day, every hour, somewhere on this planet, created beings stop their busy activity, even if only for a moment, to recognize and touch the God within all other created beings and things. And even if we are not fully aware of the divine power present in each beautiful and individual soul, each holy place or sacred moment, because of the blood of Christ we are one in communion with each other and with God, from whom all blessings flow. This meal is too large to be consumed and too good to be passed over.

# (12)

# PROFESSIONAL MINISTRY

## *a* CLAY CONDUIT
## *of* GOD'S POWER

> My problem was more than having something to say from Sunday to Sunday. My problem was what I did say had no power to help people. I had no substance, no depth. The people were starving for a word from God, and I had nothing to give them. Nothing.
>
> **Richard J. Foster**
> *Celebration of Discipline: The Path to Spiritual Growth*

The elders took turns scrounging through the cardboard box of black plastic letters in search of the vowels and consonants to correctly spell "Dan Gilliam—Evangelist." For years, the weathered sign beside Indiana State Route 52 had simply read, "Hartsville Church of Christ, Services Weekly," with no one led by God or ego to change it. Now the new young preacher sporting a fresh gray polyester suit wanted his name on the marquee, and the elders had a decision to make. Since there had been only one *m* among the grimy letters, *minister*, the preferred title of ordained leadership in the brotherhood of nondenominational Christian Churches/Churches of Christ, would not be available. I wasn't about to complain, however, for I really liked the authoritative ring of *evangelist* better. It sounded more biblical and carried some weight this skinny Bible college kid could use to make an impact at his rural weekend preaching post. It also made me feel like I was on a mission, called by God to save this heathen farming community from sin, corn liquor, and cable television. It was not as romantic a charge as missionary Jim Elliot's was—martyred by the Auca Indians he went to save—but it would do.

My part-time ministry at this midwestern country church had not been difficult to come by. A classmate of mine had grown weary of the job and had suggested my name to the church board who quickly hired me after only one sermon, the only sermon I had at the time. Initially, I accepted the terms of $50.00 per week, for which I would deliver morning and evening sermons plus a Bible school lesson. However, two weeks into it, I realized that I didn't have that much to say and fifty bucks would barely cover my fast-food meals and the gas my '74 Plymouth Duster would need for the weekly 300-mile round-trip. So, I asked the church for a twenty-five-dollar raise, begged out of the Sunday school class, and turned the Sunday night service into a "Singspiration," where people took turns yelling out page numbers— "79!" and "138!"—to songs such as "Bringing in the Sheaves" and "Blessed Assurance" from their beloved, yellowed hymnals. I would not be lying if I told you that the thought of having "Dan Gilliam—Evangelist" engraved on the hymnals had crossed my mind.

More money and less responsibility made it possible for me to stay with that ministry for my entire senior year of school until a more sizable church picked me up in the first round of my class draft and I was "called" to a big-city, suburban youth ministry. I think I might have stayed on to be the full-time preacher for the little country church, but not one of my trusted friends or college professors seemed to think it was worth considering. The consensus was that I had too many talents to waste at a small country church. While in some religious circles the precedent has been established that God only calls pastors to leave their present ministries for larger churches with better salary packages, I would later learn that doing God's will could also mean working with fewer people for less money and no health insurance.

But on that inaugural night of my first ministry, I lay wide awake, tossing on the mildewed couch in the damp pastor's study. Much like Don Knotts's character Luther Heggs in Disney's *The Ghost and Mr. Chicken*, who stayed overnight in the haunted house for the sake of a story, I was restless and edgy in my sleeping bag. Every creak and groan in the sanctuary beneath my office convinced me that Satan was lurking and roaming about in the pitch-black house of God. Perhaps it was my lingering childhood fears of the devil and the dark that motivated me to kneel that night in the sanctuary and pray at every pew. I hardly knew the faces of those who sat in their same seats each week, much less their names, but at every place, I asked God to bless their souls and do his will in their lives. While my intentions were good, and I believe God always answers prayer, that night I carried the mistaken notion that God would depend on *me* to do my ministry job well so that he could bless the helpless and hapless parishioners. I had a ways to go before I would learn that God didn't always need preachers to speak to his people, and that Sunday wasn't the only day he spoke. It was at this little "church in the wildwood" that God would reveal to me for the first of many times that neither did he need his messengers to be anything special or anywhere near perfect for holy communication to take place. God doesn't have to shout over our humanity in order to be heard by the people we seek to influence. In fact, he often favors speaking right through it, preferring God-centered, real-life stories of painful failure and redemption to self-centered testimonies and polished, pious speeches.

Perhaps it was the time I locked myself in the bathroom just minutes before my sermon was to begin; or the time I drove off with the antique silver home communion set on the roof of my car, losing it in a roadside cornfield, that blew what I perceived as my perfect image. It might also have been the Sunday I arrived as church was letting out, having missed the daylight savings time change; or my innocent use of a colorful expletive during a sermon illustration, that highlighted my humanity. More dramatically, when after only four years I resigned from my youth ministry due to an addiction to prescription medication, I showed the little world in which I lived that I was still a work in progress. Though it may have been difficult for me to see at the time, it has always been obvious to the congregations

I have served that it was not my talents or gifts for ministry that have made my clay vessel a successful conduit for God's love and power. It was his grace.

One of the things I like most about vocational or volunteer ministry, whether in the church, on the street, or in the coffee shop, is that it forces me to rely on God for the humility and unconditional love necessary to be effective in God's work. As I am a selfish man-child who still suffers from the human condition, these are attitudes I am incapable of generating within myself. Reaching out to others, with their souls' best interest in mind, requires me to take regular stock of my own spiritual condition and to trust God that his light and life will shine through my ego-inflated persona. This takes time, attention, and a deep-seated belief that I do not know what I am doing in spite of all my education, training, and experience. If I do not make the effort to seek the nurture of my heart and spirit through a regular encounter with and surrender to the Master, then I have nothing real to offer the God-seekers in my life other than secondhand stories of things I have only heard to be true. This is true for anyone who, by faith, embraces the work of the ministry.

And it has never been more true for me than now. New to professional, located ministry again after a twenty-year hiatus, I find myself with a unique opportunity to minister from my gifts, experiences, and passions as minister of meditation and prayer at LifeBridge Christian Church in Longmont, Colorado. This job description, which much to my delight I was invited to help write, calls me to help lead the staff and congregation in focusing on their inner life journey and in developing a deeper sense of intimacy with God. Practically speaking, I am charged with creating opportunities and facilitating gatherings that highlight centering prayer and shared meditation. As this is something that has captured my imagination and for many years has been a significant part of my own spiritual trek, I have no shortage of incentive for continuing to press into these contemplative and, some would say, mystical means of experiencing God's presence.

How many staff or church members will willingly follow my lead into this ancient but future practice of exploring the contemplative dimension of the gospel (as Thomas Keating would call it) is yet to be seen. Determining or predicting what others will do is not what I would consider to be part of the job. Only God can stir hearts and manifest the willingness to seek a relationship with him. Each man and woman is responsible for his or her faithfulness to God, whatever that looks like for him or her. I can only model and suggest what works for me—intentionally taking time each day to listen, love, and learn from Christ, as he makes himself known through Scripture, Spirit, and silence. In a world that hurries to get out of its own way in a time when more is better and never enough, the idea of slowing down to seek God sounds good, but feels impossible. This is a crossroads at which every Christ-follower, particularly those charged with church leadership, will have to make a decision. And while those of us in professional ministry may not need our names on a church sign to be effective evangelists or pastors to God's family of messed-up people, we will need daily conscious contact with him if we are to keep from locking ourselves in the bathroom when it is time to preach, or live, our sermons.

# ( 13 )

# PRAYER

## SWEATY PALMS
## *and* RED ROVER

Very few of us feel that we know how to pray as we ought. But we do know what it is to sigh, to yearn for a deeper and more intimate relation with the One whom Jesus taught us to call *Abba*, Father. And it is good to hear that our own sighs may be our participation in the sighing of the Spirit, helping us in our weakness, as we seek to claim our identity as daughters and sons of God. In our day many are bringing their sighing hearts before God in Centering Prayer.

**Thomas. R. Ward, Jr.**
*Centering Prayer in Daily Life and Ministry*

T
he longest documented prayers in the history of Christen-
dom have occurred while people stood outdoors, being
bitten by mosquitoes, and holding sweaty hands around
a fire. As a youth minister I observed that these sacred people-rings
were revered for their effectiveness in leading kids to make decisions
for God. Thus, we circled our youth groups to pray together as often
as we could. This included every shared meal, before and after every
event, spiritual or sports-like, and at some point during every Sunday
school class or Bible study. We were serious about our circled-up God
petitions. I would estimate that, including my years as a youth and as
a youth leader, I have been a part of more than 1,000 sweaty-handed
group prayers. I'm not bragging here, just documenting my expertise
in this area. I have been a part of some prayer circles at camps and retreats where so much body fluid was exchanged through sweaty palms
that for a time we actually became one really large person, and had
to play a game of Red Rover to become separate entities again: "Red
Rover, Red Rover, send Alex on over." This added new meaning to
our song about being one in the Spirit.

Some folks, like me, have developed an aversion to lengthy group
prayers, while others have the uncanny ability to make themselves
oblivious to the discomfort and redundancy that occurs in prayer
marathons. From my experience, the purpose of some of these prayers
was to extend the sermon just given (also long and sweaty) with stories, poems, and lyrics from the *Jesus Christ Superstar* soundtrack;
breathy, emotional explanations of what exactly we were supposed
to have learned from the homily, with emphasized specifics of how
we could apply these teachings to our daily lives. Other times, these
types of prayers sounded more like directives for God, in case he
forgot how to work; prescriptions for him to fill in order to meet the
delicate, though real, needs of individuals, the local congregation,

the church at large, the president, the Republican party, and the entire planet. (For some reason, though, we never prayed for organizations such as the Sierra Club, People for the Ethical Treatment of Animals, or Amnesty International.) You can almost picture God during some of these prayers with a notepad, scribbling furiously while nodding and mumbling, "Uh-huh . . . mmm-hmmm. I'll get right on it. Anything else?"

Sometimes I catch myself practicing these same habits in private prayer. Relapsing into moments of fear or self-righteousness, I will hear myself telling God how to run my life and to help those I think need more God in their lives. Or I will catch myself saying things to God with great yearning, hoping that God really is Santa Claus (as I've always suspected), waiting to grant me my cosmic wishes from on high, if I would only ask for them in faith. While I cannot speak for others, these types of prayers have historically not been overly beneficial to my spiritual growth or sense of intimacy with God. On the other hand, the most effective verbal prayer I have regularly prayed is a piece of the Lord's Prayer, given when Christ's disciples asked him how they should pray: "Your will be done" (Matthew 6:10). Apparently, this well-known universal prayer, one I never learned until I was thirty years old (while regularly attending 12-step meetings) because my church didn't want us to do or say anything (confessing sins was another) that resembled Catholics, contains all the elements necessary to engage the God of the universe and seek his intention for our lives. In this simple prayer, we can acknowledge the sovereignty of God, admit our dependence for daily provisions and spiritual power, and seek forgiveness as well as the ability to forgive those who have harmed us; in other words, all the good God stuff we could ever want.

Since God already knows what we need, maybe we should save our breath and spend that time listening to what he wants to say to us. Or we might even consider that one of our best means of prayer might be living out the gospel in contemplation, letting our lives be a prayer that touches all of our encounters and relationships. This form of prayer allows us to offer ourselves to God to use us as part of the answer we seek in our petitions. The only problem with this form of prayer, however, is that it requires some, even much, effort on our part. Most pray-ers I know prefer that God do it all so that they can go about their business of feeling secure and happy with their stuff and situations. After all, doing it all is God's job, isn't it?

Recently, while I was meditating through the Sermon on the Mount, I was excited to stumble once again upon one of Jesus' teachings about prayer. With fresh eyes, I read, "But when you pray, go into your room, close the door and pray to your Father, who is unseen. Then your Father, who sees what is done in secret, will reward you. And when you pray, do not keep on babbling like pagans, for they think they will be heard because of their many words. Do not be like them, for your Father knows what you need before you ask him" (Matthew 6:6-8). Christ's words discouraging prayerful "babbling" gave me comfort as these days I sometimes feel as if I don't say enough actual words to God in prayer. Though in my spiritual adolescence I once ridiculed those who claimed to "pray without ceasing," I have since committed myself to developing a practice of continual prayer and have come to prefer a persistent state of contemplative prayer to occasional wordy, though hurried, mumblings in God's direction.

More specifically, I have embraced the practice of centering prayer (called abiding prayer by some, from the King James Version of John 15:7—"If ye abide in me, and my words abide in you, ye shall ask what ye will, and it shall be done unto you"): sitting with God in silence twice a day for twenty minutes, as lived and written about by Trappist monk Thomas Keating as well as other monks and ministers. This simple yet disciplined practice of daily prayer provides an opportunity for the Christ-follower to experience interior silence and to develop the innate practice of consenting to God's presence and work in his or her life. Centering prayer helps facilitate contemplative prayer, whereby we can see God in all people, places, and things. I have so greatly enjoyed these forms of prayer that I am in danger of selling out to prayer as the primary activity of ministry that I do as a church leader. I guess a church could do worse than to have one of her pastors focused exclusively on creating activities and opportunities for helping people to seek and enjoy God's presence.

If I err these days in my prayer life, it is in my brevity of speech and my lack of interest in public, vocal prayers. Far too much public prayer in Protestant worship services has a priestly or papal quality, whereby one person does all the talking to God on behalf of everyone else. Because this method is more comfortable for ministers than the stiffness of silent prayer, we have embraced it as our primary means of praying in church. Moreover, we mistakenly believe that most references in Scripture to prayer pertain to this kind of one-way vocal exchange with God; whereby one man, preferably an ordained one, does all the talking and God is relegated to the role of listener. This is also our model for prayers before meals, which interestingly enough have become so important that many Christians cannot eat their food without verbally saying grace. Silent prayer, even in this circumstance, is for some reason considered by many to be inferior to having a designated out-loud pray-er step up and deliver the grateful goods to God so that the food will be blessed and those sitting nearby will know of our belief in God. There was a time when I thought that saying public prayers was an opportunity to display my faith and a chance to testify with courage in the presence of pagans or the spiritually weak. These days, my thoughts are more along the lines that indiscreet public prayer can sometimes appear showy and self-righteous, and bystanders are sometimes left to feel uncomfortable.

Though I enjoy formally praying the Lord's Prayer several times a week out loud with others in a (sometimes sweaty) hand-holding circle, and I regularly mutter "Your will be done" many times a day under my breath, prayer for me has for the most part become a private thing that does not require many words at all. As a form of meditation, centering prayer helps one to better understand the oft-quoted Psalm 46:10, "Be still, and know that I am God," and leads one into holistic communication with God that integrates body, soul, and spirit into the process along with the mind. When practiced in a group with other believers, centering prayer is also a significant means of building community, even without much conversation occurring. Inviting God to have his way with us leads to deeper intimacy with him and bonds us with our fellow participants. Moreover, as centering prayer opens into contemplative prayer, it becomes the best formula I have come across yet for actually praying without ceasing. Not only is it painless, it is a method of being present with God that grows more and more appealing as one practices it. Imagine that. Enjoyable prayer. It sure beats the windy, one-man, group prayers. Although I do not believe there is anything inherently wrong with long vocal prayers, to this day when I hear someone pray in public for more than thirty seconds, my palms start sweating profusely and I can hear clearly, echoing down the halls of my memory, "Red Rover, Red Rover, send Danny on over!"

# (14)

# TOUGH LOVE

## LETTING GO *and* LETTING GOD

Speaking of the British bulldog, Churchill told the audience, "The nose of the bulldog has been turned backwards so that he can breathe without letting go."

**Martin Gilbert**
*Churchill: A Life*

At sixteen years old, I could have won hands down the "worst case scenario" teen pageant (had there been one). Reeling from my parents' divorce and my painful junior high separation from friends and school, I was awash in a sea of bitterness and defiance that surprised everyone in my life, including me. My first drink of Boone's Farm Strawberry Hill wine opened a Pandora's box of genetic alcoholism that would not see a full remission until 1989. I quit or was kicked out of three high schools my sophomore year, was arrested several times on truancy, drug, and larceny charges, and spent six months behind bars in a maximum-security juvenile facility. Upon my release, I began a two-year disappearing hitchhiker act that took me from coast to coast several times and in and out of Canada and Mexico without any identification.

While most of this period is a blur, I can recall a few highlights (so to speak), such as the beating I took from a Georgia cop when, having been asked for ID, I showed him a dollar bill and told him I was George Washington. On another occasion, after I had passed out, a friend who was carrying me on his shoulder dropped me on my head but failed to tell me about it, leaving me with unexplained double vision for a week due to a serious concussion. Then there was the time a truck driver woke me up, kicking me in the ribs because I had rolled out onto the highway after passing out drunk beside the road. How I lived to tell these stories is a mystery to me. But I believe that a providential hand was upon my shoulder that was allowed to work in my life because all the people that cared about me let go and let God.

Since achieving long-term, one-day-at-a-time sobriety, it has been my privilege and duty to share my recovery experience, strength, and hope with many who have wanted to help friends or family members with similar problems. (I tried to help struggling people before this but, oddly enough, my alcoholic outreach seems to be more effective since practicing it sober.) As a rule, people who struggle with alcoholism or addictions to any of its dirty little cousins (overeating, pornography, gambling, etc.), most often have the best intentions and believe it when they tell you that this time they really mean to change. The problem, however, lies in the addict's inability to convert these sparkling intentions into life-changing actions. This is not something anyone can do for the addict, and the process by which this is learned is painful for all involved. Much heartbreak occurs when, by their deeds, our loved ones prove that they don't really want to change, in spite of what they might tell themselves and us. Christ himself had many followers who made the decision to turn their backs on him and run from the truth (see John 6:66—strange numbers considering this is the same John who wrote Revelation); so it is important that we not blame ourselves for the rebellious and sick choices of others. It is equally important not to take credit for any progress we see in the lives of those who might be in the process of growing up around us. It is only by the grace of God that anything good happens.

In advising people who are facing the dilemma of how to help an alcoholic or drug addict, I have always reverted to two simple steps (though the alcoholic may require twelve) that seem to be at the heart of the solution. First, I have seen much value in the grace and discipline of prayer. In prayer, we are reminded of our own powerlessness over most of what occurs in life, especially in the lives of others. It allows us to turn the burden of responsibility for others over to the one who is equipped to handle it. In my estimation, that's what prayer is about: releasing results to God and trusting God for outcomes.

A second effective tool is the process of letting go with love. This is sometimes hard to define, but it primarily involves leaving our lost loved ones to their own devices so that they can experience the full weight of the consequences of their actions. We don't do anyone with a behavior problem a favor when we soften the blows or hinder them from hitting the bottom that could very well shake them to their senses. For me, this meant that my friends and family had to say "We love you, but we will no longer tolerate your behavior. When you are ready to do something different, come back and we will walk with you. But if you continue on your current path then you need to go away." Harsh words indeed, but ones that saved my life. I am one of the fortunate ones who has been given another opportunity at living life. Many do not receive this.

There are no guarantees that our wayward friends will return or survive themselves, but we can find assurance in knowing that we did all we could to help. Most often, however, this feels to be very little. When we release our self-suffering brothers and sisters to themselves, we do so with the hopes that they will experience the pain of their fall and return quickly for another taste of grace. (This was the apostle Peter's story.) I wonder if Christ was practicing tough love with Judas Iscariot when he said to him at the Last Supper, "What you are about to do, do quickly" (John 13:27). Unfortunately, the weight of Judas's remorse was too great for him to handle and he took his own life. This is not an unusual scenario, particularly for those who have once known the truth and then left it for other courses. There is no easy solution in helping the helpless and we have no real choice but to let go of them with love.

Tough love is just that. Tough to give, tough to take, but it is powerful and it represents our last line of defense. It is helpful to remember that we are not the only agents God will use in the lives of our loved ones. There will be others, and we will have to trust the same God who lovingly and persistently works in our lives to do the same work in the lives of others. We are individually but links in the chain of godly influence that transforms attitudes and changes minds in the face of intense resistance and horrendous odds. It is an arrogant error to overestimate the impact that any one person can have on someone else. We must also keep in mind that God's time-table is never easy to understand and impossible to estimate. As far as we know, God doesn't carry a watch or a sundial, so we might save ourselves the trouble of sitting around waiting for God to answer our prayers, particularly when we are praying for someone with a hardened heart. Sometimes devastation and trouble can be the very bad-tasting medicine that softens our calloused spirits so that we can desire and pursue the good stuff of God. This infinite grace and un-ending love is available for any and all who seek it, even if the search is only as wide as a keyhole and the interest as large as a mustard seed. I'm banking on the hope that if this formula for letting go with love could work on a teenage drunk with a concussion that used an alias like George Washington, it can work for anyone.

# ( 15 )

# BIBLE COLLEGE

## SUNDAY SCHOOL *for* FUTURE *and* FAILED SAINTS

Saints become saints by somehow hanging on to the stubborn conviction that things are not as they appear, and that the unseen world is as solid and trustworthy as the visible world around them. God deserves trust, even when it looks like the world is caving in.

**Philip Yancey**
*Disappointment with God: Three Questions No One Asks Aloud*

When I enrolled in Cincinnati Bible College in the fall of 1978, I had obviously not traveled the path of the typical freshman to get there. I perceived (perhaps wrongly) that most of the new CBC students had come directly from distinguished high school careers where they had been honored as Outstanding Young Students of America and were elected as presidents of their church youth groups. In contrast, I was a high school dropout. Some CBC students had excelled in Bible Bowl competitions and participated in preaching contests at Christian teen conventions. I was a master hitchhiker and an expert at bumming spare change from total strangers. Prior to coming to Bible college, most of my fellow students had been living responsible lives at home, enjoying family relationships and encouraging friendships with other Christians. I had been living under bridges in the company of bums, drunks, and perverts, playing my guitar on street corners for food and dope money. Many of CBC's students had been bright spots in their communities, making their parents, churches, and towns proud to send one of their own off to study for a career in God's service. I was no town's favorite son and had been escorted to many city limits and county lines by police, with warnings never to return. In spite of my rough road there, I arrived at CBC fresh from a spiritual awakening that had been given to me in part through one of God's long-haired freaky people who happened to be passing out Christian tracts in downtown Tampa, Florida. Through a Bible verse as simple and familiar as John 3:16, God broke my heart and led me home to make a new start at life.

In the first months following my conversion, I was hungry for all the worship and fellowship I could eat and naturally gravitated toward the Holy Roller, Jesus-people-type gatherings that were popular in the late 1970s. Their high-spirited testimonials and fresh

God music were very appealing to wide-eyed, low-bottom converts like me and gave me context for the excitement I was feeling about my new life in Christ. I found these Spirit-filled people exhilarating to be around, and my creative juices flowed into new songs, poems, and drawings that all reflected my recent return to faith. Those close to me, however, urged me not to get too involved with "those people." The problem with the Pentecostal-type celebrations, according to my well-informed Christian church friends (including a girlfriend with much hormonal influence over me), was that they tended to have charismatic leanings and were not sound in their doctrine. It was better, they inferred, to have more of an intellectual and balanced practice of faith than to be caught up in a shallow, emotional experience (not to be confused with a shallow, intellectual experience). Besides, as all believers know, Satan can disguise himself as an angel of light, and there was no telling but that some of those supernatural healings and heavenly tongue-speakings might just be "of the devil." If I was to seek God's will for my life and be sure that I was on the right road, I was told I should do it within the confines of the scriptural interpretations taught by our "movement," and that I should let the Bible be my source for any Holy Spirit guidance or leading. Almost thirty years later, I am still in search of the living balance that honors both inspired scriptural direction and a sensitivity to Holy Spirit guidance.

As it seemed best at the time, I took the shirttail-tugging advice of my friends and ministers and settled down in my expressions of faith. In no time, I learned to swim in the conservative stream of the independent Christian Churches and Churches of Christ and embraced for myself the way we viewed the things of God. If that "old time religion" was good enough for the Hebrew children, Paul and Silas, and our minister, then it certainly ought to be good enough for me. And it was. There, in the closest thing I've ever known to a home church, I found my fit historically, relationally, and theologically. It felt good to be loved and accepted in the congregation of my family's heritage, where my ninety-year-old grandmother still sang in the choir and where I was known as "Charlie and Ann's boy." It felt right to reunite with friends I had known for years, though I had been the terminal backslider for whom they had often prayed. Now I was hanging out with the guys who had prayed for me, throwing strikes and gutter balls at the Christian bowling alley, eating subs and pizza after Sunday night church, and singing out loud with the Beach Boys en route to "calling" on other perpetual sinners. Life was pretty good for me and I credited it all to God. Within months, I would feel the nagging desire to be more and do more for this God of second chances. Thanks to some area youth ministers I admired, namely Jerry Odell and Kevin Odor, and my church's policy of paying for four years of Bible college tuition, I made the decision in the summer of 1978 to dedicate my life to full-time Christian service.

One of the first CBC students I met at freshman orientation was Rich Mullins, the soon-to-be heralded contemporary Christian singer/songwriter. Accompanied by his vocal group, Zion, Rich was performing some of his new songs, such as "Sing Your Praise to the Lord" and "Hope to Carry On." I found myself drawn to this guy who dressed and talked like I did when I was living on the streets, but who seemed to know quite a bit about the life and teachings of Jesus. While no one ever came out and said it, the school's unofficial stance on Rich was that he was a spiritual anarchist who sometimes had some profound things to say about God, but who didn't think any of the school's guidelines applied to him. (In his defense, I think that this reputation had more to do with his unwillingness to comply with a "no jeans in class" dress code and the fact that he played the practice pianos harder than the music professors preferred.) Most of the students thought Rich's music and lyrics were borderline inspiring and it was generally assumed that he lived in the neighborhood of the holy life because he sang so many songs about it. However, he did not try to hide the fact that he was made of very human raw material, and he would let this show on campus from time to time.

One day I came out of my dorm laundry room just in time to hear Rich cussing out some guy with the three-syllable name that every major league baseball player and manager knows will get you thrown out of the game if you use it on an umpire. (Watch the movie *Bull Durham* if you need more on this.) After that episode, I never had any notions about Rich Mullins being a saint, but neither did he. It would be a couple more years before I would fall hard again and learn why sainthood is reserved for people who have been dead a long time. After you're dead and buried, there is no one left to remember all the human stains you got on your God stories while you were alive. People tend to want to remember only the good stuff. Rich Mullins would find it hilarious to know that, since his fatal auto accident in 1997, people have already cleaned up the memory and record of his ragamuffin life. It is ironic that in spite of his best efforts to avoid it, Rich has become a saint.

Because of the crooked path I had traveled to get to Bible college, I was not impressed with Rich's or anyone else's reputation for being a rebel. I felt that I had done the sinner thing full throttle and that anyone who claimed to be a Christian should do his or her best in trying to live the life that Jesus lived. In retrospect, I think I believed for a period of time that I was actually immune to sin, and keeping this delusion alive was more important than coming to terms with the truth about my humanity. I didn't yet have a place for what it meant to be an honest sinner in the hands of a loving God. I related better to Jonathan Edwards's much-esteemed sermon entitled "Sinners in the Hands of an Angry God." And when you are in the business of condemning yourself for not being good enough in God's eyes, no one else is allowed to measure up either. While a few students and some of the faculty were tapping into the realities of being free in Christ, the rest of us were busy perpetuating legalistic messages that "right living" somehow positively influenced God's opinion of us. In our heads we knew that it was Christ who made us righteous, and that even if we still had a sin-streak a mile wide, God could not love us any less. But it was hard to get this message to travel the long and winding road eighteen inches south into our heart of hearts. To this day, I meet people who have spent a lifetime in church but who have yet to believe and accept the unbelievable message of grace. It's just too good to be true, isn't it?

Though some of my most painful (though effective) reality lessons about stilted sainthood were still a few years away, I had a great experience at Cincinnati Bible College (now Cincinnati Christian University). Surrounded by many who took their faith seriously, as well as some who did not, I learned to function as a vital part of the body of Christ. I embraced every opportunity to worship, serve, and grow that was available to me. My years of surviving as a street troubadour prepared me unknowingly to be a regular in the school's traveling ministry and recruitment teams. I traveled every weekend during the school year and spent my summers at camps and conferences, leading worship, sharing my testimony, and polishing my preaching and teaching skills.

The more I gave of myself, the more I believed that God had hand-selected me for the professional ministry and, whether this was true or not, in 1980, Northside Church of Christ (now Northside Christian Church) in Newport News, Virginia, ordained me to God's service as a minister of the gospel. And though my journey has had many unexpected twists and turns since that day, I believe I have always been a vessel in God's hands for touching the lives of others with his miraculous message. Contrary to what I believed or was taught in my Christian college education, God seems to prefer to minister through me more out of my brokenness than through my giftedness. It is through my failings and flaws that the grace of God is released to flow into the cracks and spaces of my life. My humanity, as distasteful as it can sometimes be, allows him room to work in me and show that "we have this treasure in jars of clay to show that this all-surpassing power is from God and not from us" (2 Corinthians 4:7). And while I may have been a failure at one or more of the definitions of *saint*, perhaps a better idea of sainthood as defined in my life has been about staying true to the process of reliance upon God, no matter what I have to go through to get there.

# (16)

# PAINTING

## WHERE *the* GOD *in* ART
## MEETS *the* GOD *in* ME

All children are artists, and it is an indictment of our culture that so many of them lose their creativity, their unfettered imaginations, as they grow older. But they start off without self-consciousness as they paint their purple flowers, their anatomically impossible people, their thunderous, sulphurous skies. They don't worry that they may not be as good as Di Chirico or Bracque; they know intuitively that it is folly to make comparisons, and they go ahead and say what they want to say.

**Madeleine L'Engle**
*Walking on Water: Reflections on Faith and Art*

The last time I saw Rich Mullins was in July of 1994. I was performing and speaking at Christ In Youth conferences that summer and I heard that Rich would be doing a concert in nearby Springfield, Missouri. I called ahead to alert my old friend and former youth ministry intern, Dave Strasser (aka Beaker), that I would be coming so that I would be sure to get some time with him and maybe even get into the show without paying. Arriving early, I found Dave milling about backstage, and he eagerly introduced me around to a few crew members and some of the Ragamuffin band (Jimmy Abegg and Rick Elias). Though Rich's concert was enjoyable, I was more affected by seeing the crew painting with watercolors backstage. They seemed to be simply playing with the colors, no one expecting anything profound to occur—just enjoying the experience. These young adults were tapping into the energy and imagination that most of us leave behind at childhood. I asked Dave about it, for I was immediately fascinated and heard myself saying aloud, "I want to do that!" His simple advice to me would influence my life in ways that I still cannot fully comprehend. All he told me was to go buy the cheapest watercolor paper, paint, and brush that I could find and, "See what happens." I could never have known what a faith crawl I was about to experience through the lands of color, shape, beauty, and divine desire. I will always be grateful to Rich and Beaker for introducing me to the touch of God through painting.

Anyone who knows me can fill in the blanks with what happened next, for I have since sold over a hundred original canvasses that now hang in homes and offices in many states including Oregon, Arizona, California, Ohio, Virginia, Indiana, and North Carolina, as well as in several other countries including Italy, Australia, and Canada. Painting has become not only an important part of my identity but a vital tool in my kit for spiritual health. Something about getting lost in the timeless universe of creativity helps me bring balance into an otherwise frenetically paced world. I never intended for art to be a financial enterprise—which is a good thing, since selling paintings has never been predictable and is rarely profitable. But I found that when I strategically placed pictures on the stage behind me to add a colorful backdrop to the set, every once in a while someone would walk up after the concert with a blank stare and a checkbook, signifying the desire to buy one of my paintings. I am delighted to know that somewhere tonight my artwork adorns the walls, shelves, and fireplace mantles of people who found beauty in something I created because it made me feel closer to God.

In faith, I kneel down in front of what was once a nightstand for a 1980s waterbed suite and pull out my paints, paper, palette knife, and masking tape. This is the throne at which I bow to seek and experience God. Having lit a stick of patchouli incense and launched a CD of instrumental music, I have a general idea of what I am about to do, though there is an element of mystery regarding the outcome. The fact that I have been here before does little to calm my suspicions that I am doomed to fail in this venture and that my efforts to produce a pleasing piece of art will leave me dissatisfied and drained. I play a game with my expectation-laden mind, tricking it into thinking that I am just out to have fun and that in no way am I trying to create something meaningful and beautiful. I attempt to let the fear-riddled thoughts pass me by as if they were coal-loaded barges laboring up the Mississippi River, acknowledging that "There they are," and then "There they go." If I were to wait for all unpleasant feelings and insecurities to be gone before I set out to create, I would never begin anything. It is in the action of picking up the palette knife or the paintbrush that I begin my journey into the presence of God.

By faith, and with a mysterious mixture of intention and detachment, I choose my colors and begin to squeeze generous dabs onto my eagerly awaiting canvas. Intuitively, my hands begin to work the paint back and forth, not unlike spreading peanut butter on a piece of warm toast. I am in search of some sort of combination of line, texture, and blend of pigments that will be delightful to my eye and delicious to my psyche. The trick is to recognize when it is time to stop; when one more stroke—the unnecessary one—would turn magic into mud. (They say it takes two people to paint a picture: one to paint and one to hit the painter with a brick to let him know he's finished.)

By the time I arrive at my finishing point ten minutes, two days, or two weeks later, I am no longer painting with my cognitive mind but my spirit, heart, and hand have formed a partnership with the great force beyond me yet inside of me. This is creative energy—the Christ Spirit behind the creation of all things communicating in spite of, but through, me. I become a channel through which the God in art meets the God in me. If by chance you see my painting, or another's, and are open to the voice of God—the same voice that created the world and everything in it—then the God in you might see the God in art and bow in acknowledgment of this creative handiwork. Most of my Christian friends aren't sure what to say about all this, but I am getting used to the idea that Christianity is bigger than many Christians seem to know or want to believe.

Painting also is more than many might understand or admit. It is not reserved for the talented or the dope smoker, and not everyone who is into painting is gay or mentally unbalanced, though there are plenty of all of these who regularly create in this medium. In my own journey I have discovered that painting is often a metaphor for how I live life. There are not very many days where I really know what lies ahead for me. Although my appointment book might be full, I cannot see ahead to know what glimpses I will get into the nature of God each day or what surprises will come to me through the least expected sources. As in painting, I have to trust and pick up the brushes of my life to see what delightful or disconcerting picture I will participate in making each day. Some are certainly better than others, and there is no rule saying I can't scrap the whole thing and start over if one of my days isn't working for me.

I'm looking at a painting right now that I have been trying to make beautiful for about a month and I'm pretty sure that tomorrow it will end up in the dumpster. But the process has not been wasted, regardless of the final product; for out of my "failed" experiment I got an idea for a chapter in this book you are now reading. It doesn't matter what anyone else thinks of my paintings—when they are finished or while they are a work in progress—for if all they are is part of the process by which I feel the touch of God they are worthy efforts indeed. Who cares that I have to kill a canvas to get to this point? It's part of the journey, and in God's economy, nothing is wasted. So why don't you take Beaker's advice: buy the cheapest watercolor set you can find and "see what happens." You might paint a masterpiece, decorate your refrigerator, or even throw your picture away and write a book. Or you might simply open your eyes to see that you've been painting your life for years and didn't even know it.

# ( 17 )

# PICTURES

## STAINED-GLASS
## WINDOWS
## *and* JUDAS'S KISS

His main efforts went into a few very large paintings, on each of which he spent a year's time or more. One reason why he worked so slowly was his belief that art ought to be based on a "system"; like Degas, he had studied with a follower of Ingres, and his interest in theory came from this experience. But as with all artists of genius, Seurat's theories do not explain his pictures; it is the pictures, rather, that explain the theories.

**H. W. Janson and Dora Jane Janson**
*The Picture History of Painting:*
*From Cave Painting to Modern Times*

A few years ago, a friend of mine who happened to be living in a restored cathedral in Cincinnati, Ohio, invited me to perform a concert there. Undergoing a transformative renovation, Saint George Church was making a comeback that old George himself and Rome, Italy, likely knew little about. On the verge of demolition in the late 1990s, this 130-year-old former monastery had recently become a haven to a variety of nonprofit groups and grass roots organizations. She was also apparently the recipient of generous historical grants and was the darling of projects deemed worth funding among the well-heeled. Along with the world's only known sacristy (a room where sacred vessels and vestments were kept) coffee bar, The George, as she was affectionately called by her live-in staff, also housed a first-rate religious bookstore. Shadowlands, one of the more visible and active nonprofits, was a street-level ministry designed to touch unreached and over-churched young adults with the love of God and the thump of hard-core music. Along with his merry band of part-time and volunteer wunderkinds willing to work for minimum wage, coffee, and day-old bread, the twenty-something director organized concerts, art shows, service projects, and any number of unlikely gatherings for postmodern and pre-pastoral college-age kids. I can't say that I know much about the original sainted George, but his hip and holy namesake in Cincinnati might certainly have made him proud.

Other than the humble and modish ministry servants, the cavernous bell towers, and the mahogany-lined, prayer-soaked monk cells, my favorite features of Old Saint George are the twelve gorgeous stained-glass windows that picture the life of Christ, beginning with the annunciation and ending with the ascension. These vibrant masterpieces climb nearly to the top of the 80-foot ceilings with majestic flair, showering all who pass below with colors and stories of the biblical God. For any passersby with the time to pause for reflection and meditation there awaits an imaginative glimpse into the otherworldliness of Christ and his first followers. As in the Dark Ages, when illiteracy abounded and pictures and statues became commonplace in the church, those windows may have been the best look some of Old Saint George's homeless and hurting clientele (not to mention the rich and agnostic patrons) got at the story of Jesus Christ.

Like many before me, the first of my spiritual awakenings occurred while studying the stained-glass windows of my childhood church. There, in the Garden of Gethsemane, I understood the anguish of the pleading Christ and felt the heavy eyelids of the prayed-out disciples. In the same breath, I too, gave my heart to Jesus and fell asleep moments later in a nap of unfaithfulness. While the words of *The Living Bible* and the song lyrics of Cat Stevens and Harry Chapin taught me many of life's important lessons, it is likely that growing up I learned as much or more from the creative pictures of Peter Max, Ansel Adams, and LeRoy Neiman. When my dad's sermons went long and the grand old hymns became redundant, I would cast my gaze upward and explore the rich worlds of olive and ultramarine, ochre and crimson that made up these action-filled scenes from the life of Jesus. On a clear Sunday morning, when sunbeams backlit the tinted glass panes, I could almost smell the bread and wine of the Last Supper and feel the breath of Christ on my face as he filled his disciples with the Holy Spirit.

One of the hazards of living next to the church building when I was growing up was that from time to time I would get into trouble due to treating the church as an extension of our parsonage. During my entire childhood I never mastered the art of considering the consequences before taking the actions that got me into trouble. I just did things and learned to pay the price if I broke something or missed the mark of perfection in some way. Therefore, it should have been no big surprise to anyone who knew me that the day would come when I would throw a baseball through one of the fifty-year-old stained-glass windows on the side of the church. I didn't mean to. I was just playing catch with myself because my parents refused to have any more male children after me, and my three sisters had no interest in America's pastime. That day, my breaking ball refused to break and instead went crashing through the betrayal scene on the Mount of Olives just where Jesus was being arrested and Peter was drawing his sword. The following Sunday morning, people were surprised to see the hole of light that mysteriously appeared where Judas's lips once puckered to kiss Jesus. Hearing the buzz of comments during the service, I thought for a while that I might actually be honored for my errant throw, as the word *miracle* was used by one elderly woman to describe the incident. I was not so lucky. Instead, my allowance was held back for a year or so to pay for the damage and I never did develop much of a curve ball. But that's another story.

Losing myself in the pictured chronicles of windows and Bibles not only helped me to grasp the divinity of the Son of God but also helped free me from the scary bonds of misunderstood eternity. *Forever* was a very big subject in our church and it was used every Sunday to motivate people to rededicate their lives to Christ or to give more money to the building fund. There was never much talk of days or years back then; things happened either for eternity or not at all. *Forever* carried a lot of weight. Like when your parents told you that if you crossed your eyes one time too many, they would be stuck like that forever. A week or a month of a stuck, cross-eyed face would never have scared anyone into straightening up, but *forever* got your attention. Apparently, in church, use of the word *forever* was designed to make Hell seem hotter and Heaven smell sweeter, but no one I knew was very interested in the idea of doing the same thing for more than an hour or two, much less for the rest of time. The only things we wanted to last forever were Christmas, Easter, and Halloween—the sugar-based holidays. And the only thing that interested me about eternity was the possibility that Heaven included an endless supply of candy. Hell, of course would be candy-less. Forever.

In pictures, however, there is no beginning or end, only the currently viewed version of now. Therefore, when staring at stained-glass windows or flipping through the color photographs and topographic maps in my *Revised Standard Version* Bible, a restless kid like me could dawdle and take some time to think about things. Past and present, as tools for measuring time, life, or God, do not exist in images. There is no pressure to understand anything or to make any hurried decisions. In pictures, life isn't going anywhere and one does not have to hurry to catch up with it. Gazing at storied windows and Bible pictures as a child allowed me to see God without any expectation that I would understand him. I could simply pause to look and believe and that was good enough. Even today, this tool of grace comes in handy when I want a bit of God without having to think too much about it. I can bask in the presence of a God moment simply by taking the time to study the stories of a world full of drawings, paintings, mosaics, collages, or photographs, all of which can speak magical and eternal truths without uttering a single word.

# (18)

# WORK

## *from* PAPER BOY
## *to* STARVING ARTIST

"Business!" cried the Ghost, wringing its hands again. "Mankind was my business. The common welfare was my business; charity, mercy, forbearance, and benevolence, were, all, my business. The dealings of my trade were but a drop of water in the comprehensive ocean of my business!"

**Charles Dickens**
*A Christmas Carol*

I was nine years old in the summer of 1968 when, at the urging of my father, I went door to door in search of neighbors willing to pay a kid to cut their lawns. It wasn't hard to know who to ask, I simply started with the yards sporting knee-high grass, weeds and dandelions. Being a smart kid, I soon figured out that several of these yards belonged to families whose teenage boys—the ones who usually cut the grass—were far away in a place called Vietnam. One boy on our street never came home from there, and his shiny orange Pontiac ("here comes the") Judge with double black stripes sat in front of his house until the wide racing tires went flat. For that and many other reasons, there was plenty of work to be had that summer and before long, I was riding my bike to other streets and neighborhoods—my rusted-red Briggs and Stratton mower with matching one-gallon gas can in tow. Though I despised trimming around trees and beside sidewalks, I just loved the freshly cut patterns that fell behind me as I methodically and hypnotically pushed my mower across the yards. The smell of newly mown grass and cut wild onions (mingled with strains of gasoline) were comforting scents that to this day remind me that life is beautiful and school is out for the summer.

As the seasons changed and our neighborhood yard games turned from baseball to football, my jobs also shifted, and in 1969, I got my own paper route. Any romantic notions I had of being a paper boy, fueled by television episodes of *Leave It to Beaver* and comic book issues of *Archie*, quickly dissolved into the realities of hard work and commitment. After school, when other kids were playing sports or watching TV, I was hard at work—folding, carrying, and delivering newspapers. Sometimes I could intimidate my sisters into helping me by shooting rubber bands at them, but for the most part, I was on my own. Loaded down with a front-and-rear-pouch newspaper bag, I climbed aboard my trusty Sting-Ray bicycle and pedaled furiously for what seemed like miles before arriving at my designated route. There, with expert timing and precision, I pitched my newspapers with side-armed strikes that crashed into aluminum screen doors and made barking dogs and crying children run for cover. Occasionally, I would have to stop to retrieve an errant toss from the shrubs or a flower bed, but for the most part I slipped through the neighborhood unnoticed, like an invisible superhero on a stealth mission. Each day, in my own little competitive imagination, I finished my route in record time and afterwards settled into the family couch for a well-deserved dose of Oreos and milk while watching the latest adventures of Johnny Quest and Ultraman.

In the heart of a bitterly cold winter, paper routes cease to be either fun or glamorous. On more than one occasion, I remember looking up at the downtown bank clock in Manhattan, Kansas, to see the temperature flashing minus three degrees. My hands would be solidly numb and my studded bicycle tires would barely cut through the drifts of snow and ice that the plows had thrown to the side of the road. The word *frostbite* came to my mind with surprising frequency during the days we were struck by a blizzard, as did repeated thoughts about death. I was convinced that if I stopped pedaling for even a second I would freeze in midair, like a cartoon character shot with some kind of atomic ice gun. Climbers of Mount Everest could not attest to any worse conditions. The only thing that could make the life of a paper boy worse in the dead of winter was having to deliver his papers before sunup on Sunday morning. On many a dangerously cold, first-day dawn, my mom—with winter coat covering her house coat—literally saved my life by taking me out to my route in the family's Mercury station wagon. To this day, Mom often refers to that time of our lives as when she had a part-time paper route. It never occurred to me to share my profits with her. But then, I'm not sure she would have been all that excited about the black licorice and *Mad* magazines on which I spent most of my money.

I have heard it said that the average man or woman works at three careers over the course of his or her lifetime. Not counting my two childhood jobs, by the ripe age of twenty-nine I had already cycled through my three allotted careers: house framer, youth minister, and car salesman. I don't remember much about the framing job as I went to work high most days. Not too smart when you consider how often we walked across two-inch beams three stories above the ground. The youth ministry was my dream job, not only because I got paid to eat pizza, watch movies, and camp out a lot, but because I got to do it all in the name of providing spiritual direction to teens. After (rightly) getting fired for relapsing into alcoholism and drug addiction, selling cars was my natural next career step. Ex-ministers like me often find themselves with a sales job, in part because we have a line to use with potential buyers to gain their confidence: "Hey, you can trust me. I used to work for God." Unfortunately, some of us then proceed to sell them overpriced furniture, carpet, or automobiles that they would often regret buying before they were paid for. I lasted six months in car sales and, needless to say, made more money than friends during that time.

When, in 1989, I entered the next chapter of work life, gratefully defined by a path of permanent sobriety, I embarked on my most satisfying occupation yet—that of self-employed (read starving) artist. To this job I have clung loosely for seventeen-plus years, interrupted only twice by temporary (until God shows me otherwise) religious employment. And while I have yet to acquire notable fortune or recognizable fame, I have sauntered and motored over large tracks of this beautiful planet, married my lovely and loving best friend, and have left in my wake a healthy body of original, though obscure, paintings, songs, and writings. I have also enjoyed much free time that has afforded me many hours and days for contemplation and meditation, reading and journaling that have aided my spiritual development and helped shape my perspective on both the human and the divine. Add to this list thousands of casual, though meaningful, acquaintances and a couple dozen treasured friendships, and anyone who cares to look can see that my labors on the dark (read ignored) side of the art, music, and writing industry moon have not been in vain.

In January of 2004, my work life took an unexpected turn. Whether the planets shifted or not, I don't know, but it became clear to me that I was immediately going to have to create something besides art to earn my keep and feed my cats. The independent retreat and concert market that had been my bread and butter for years seemed to suddenly dry up and blow away. With our slim savings account quickly withering to a pittance, my wife and I kicked into last-resort mode and went on the hunt for "regular" jobs. We had often spoken of this as our worst-case scenario and had said to each other that if my artsy, gypsy work ever went away, we could always stop traveling and get employment anywhere we decided to live. I had mistakenly figured this to be ten to twenty years up the road but with the clock now moved up, it was time for us to get busy. We remembered a few beach bums and alcoholics back on Hatteras Island, North Carolina, who made ends meet cleaning vacation rentals on weekends and had weekdays free to surf, work other jobs, or just drink. This sounded ideal to me now (except for the drinking), as I was not yet ready to give up my vocation of starving artist even if it had quit paying the bills. A phone call to a former landlord in North Cackalacky (Carolina) secured us an affordable rental cottage, and upon arrival our first interview landed us jobs as bona fide, professional housekeepers.

Within weeks, I become proficient at shining up sinks, toilets, tubs, and windows, while Lynn mastered the art of cleaning kitchens and making beds. We worked very hard to earn a week's worth of minimum wage in two days so that we could enjoy five days off for our creative and healthful pursuits (and to let our bodies heal from climbing millions of stairs). Lynn also occasionally substitute-taught at one of the two schools on the island. We didn't own much of anything or have any health insurance but we were content each day in the knowledge that God had granted us this situation for a reason and that until a different opportunity presented itself to us, this was life, and we were learning to love it. I think that's how life goes, after all, no matter what you are doing or how much money you have in the bank. There is no magic potion or position in life that can make you happy. Whether you are an heiress or a hot dog vendor, you have to get happy with the circumstances that are real and current in your life, not hold out for something better so you can be happy if and when that thing comes about.

My ideas about work are being altered with each passing day, as I no longer define myself by what I do for rent and food. While it is true that I can now add cleaning toilets to my résumé and list of careers, my real life's work happens every time I sit down to write a story or paint a picture, or every time I reach out to share my experience, strength, and hope with a suffering alcoholic. My vocation is seeking the ways and wisdom of God through spiritual writings, poetry, music, and nature. I believe my real work is being a friend to planet Earth, hungry strangers, lonely neighbors, abandoned animals, public servants, curious children, hurried vacationers, burdened parents, discouraged golfers, and burned-out pastors. The bottom line is that my work is not about me and what I want or do. It is about being available to the Spirit of the universe on a daily basis so that I can be a wide conduit for love, grace, peace, and joy to this world. On this path, I am blessed with more gifts than I could ever earn or buy with all the best-paying jobs in the world. All the while, as I cycle through money-making ventures—one after another depending on the season—it seems I get closer with each passing day to cutting grass or taking on that van-driving paper route. Wonder if my mom is busy on Sunday mornings these days?

# (19)

# DOCTRINE

## SCRIPTURE-READ,
## SPIRIT-LED,
## *and* FELLOWSHIP-FED

I believe a mature spirituality encourages personal participation. It asks each seeker to hold his spiritual "talk" up to the mirror of his real-life "walk" of personal experience. We must personally participate in the ongoing evolution of our spiritual deepening—and of our chosen religious practice. . . . We are asked to refuse to accept doctrine blindly without personal exploration.

**Joseph Sharp**
*Spiritual Maturity: Stories and Reflections
for the Ongoing Journey of the Spirit*

I have been a loser since the seventh grade. At least that's how I felt about myself for many years. All typical adolescent insecurities aside, I wore white socks long before it was cool and got my first sports letter in tennis, not football. I thought Neil Diamond and John Denver rocked—which they did, but it was not part of the junior high code of cool to dig the same musicians your mother was into. This was the same year that I took my Bible to school and actually read it in the cafeteria during lunch period. No wonder my first crush, Julie Fogerson, never would sit next to me. I was a dork with acne who wore his one favorite, Kansas State University T-shirt practically every day. Fortunately for me there were so many of us losers in the seventh grade that I don't think I stood out. Even as a loser, I was nothing special.

Now I'm an adult and I still can't seem to shake the loser tag. But that's OK, this time it's a good thing. I have grown up to embody the ultimate spiritual paradoxes of surrendering to win, losing to gain, and dying to live. I have buried the old self and am resolutely born again. As a result, I am a sparkling witness of the love of God. The miracle of transformation is upon me and I am no longer guided by the prevailing trade winds of this world. I have a larger calling to which I adhere and a higher road that I travel. From time to time, I flounder and fail, but it is not the big deal my ego would have me make of it. My humanity has not gone away, and I have ceased wishing it would. If anything, I have learned to embrace it as another way of identifying with Christ, who was also fully human in addition to being fully God. While there are times when I appear to get things right, there are also times when my arrogance, fear, cynicism, and pride present occasions for the light of Christ to shine from me and allow me to say, along with the apostle Paul,

> If you only look at us, you might well miss the brightness. We
> carry this precious Message around in the unadorned clay pots of
> our ordinary lives. That's to prevent anyone from confusing God's
> incomparable power with us. As it is, there's not much chance
> of that. You know for yourselves that we're not much to look at.
> (2 Corinthians 4:7, 8, *The Message*)

So, I'm a loser saved by grace and pretty happy about it all. My humanity, far from being an anchor that keeps me from soaring to great spiritual heights, is instead an avenue for God to showcase his grace. I have become a "slave to righteousness" which means my default behavior is now one of obedience, not because of any act of my will but because the Spirit of God lives in me. My heart is Christ's room with a view and a wood-burning fireplace.

I am confident that those with whom I travel in this venture to live out the gospel in real-time, real-life fashion want nothing more from their teachers and preachers than for us to be true to the vision and the voice that come to us directly and indirectly from God. Even when speaking our minds sounds offensive to some and divisive to others, there is a reverence that accompanies our commitment to speaking the truth as we have come to know it through the Word of God and our own spiritual experience. We trust God to communicate through our clay pots and ordinary lives as we attempt to live out the truth we teach as best we can. I suppose there will always be a tension between living out God's will and being my own crusty, cantankerous self. But I don't worry, for as long as Christ is the head of the church, it will be safe from those of us attempting to control it through our life's calling. With his watchful care and firm hand, Jesus shepherds his wayward and stubborn flock as we listen for his voice to follow. He is also capable of dishing out the smackdown to any thief who would steal his sheep by leading them with false motives and fear.

One of the ways that I have been shepherded and guided over the years has been through a Scripture-read, Spirit-led, and fellowship-fed doctrine of truth that has morphed from time to time in its applications to modern life, but has remained unchanged in its core and meaning. Many who know me are aware that I have traversed an interesting, if not radical, path of spiritual understanding and application, and some have mistakenly assumed that I have thrown out the doctrinal baby with the legalistic bathwater. Not true. Due in part to my alcoholism-related departure from the ministry in the early 1980s, for over twenty years I have enjoyed the freedom to question and test the validity and interpretations of the biblical teachings I have heard about and studied since birth. But in spite of my fearless searches for truth among many religious perspectives and points of view, as is often the case for religious prodigals like myself, I have come full circle to embrace a doctrinal plank not far from the conservative platform on which my parents, elders, and professors raised, trained, and ordained me. This system of belief, my doctrinal path to God, is as strong as tempered steel. It has been forged on the fires of personal reality and prayer and been borne from the seeds of spiritual fruit and power. I say this not because of any grand accomplishment on my part, but as Rich Mullins sang regarding his creed, "I did not make it, no it is making me."

For fully devoted God-followers, the real challenge is not in finding a doctrinal position in which we can be convicted and comfortable, but in avoiding the habit of judging those whose doctrinal paths differ from our own. "Live and let live" is a good motto for this occasion. It can help us remain open to seeing the thumbprint of God on the doctrinal stance of others while remaining true to what works for us. That said, here is a description of some of the tenets of my current doctrinal path to God.

## 1. Creation and Rebellion

I believe that God, who has lived in a state of timelessness forever, created the heavens and the earth and all that inhabit it through the ways and means of his choosing. Humans are the jewel of all his creations, made in the male and female image of God. Man was given dominion over the earth and, for a time, enjoyed a state of paradise in relationship with God until, at the urging of the fallen angel Satan, he exercised his options of sin and self-will, entering the realm of rebellion. As stated in Romans 5:12, "Sin entered the world through one man, and death through sin, and in this way death came to all men, because all sinned." This resulted in a one-way ticket for Adam and Eve out of the Garden of Eden and a separation from God that introduced death, sweat, pain, and hardship as necessary companions to the life of mankind on earth. Fortunately for all, God in his omniscience saw this coming from the start and made arrangements for our return to relationship with him through the sacrificial gift of his Son. "Just as through the disobedience of the one man the many were made sinners, so also through the obedience of the one man the many will be made righteous" (Romans 5:19). Man returns to a relationship with God through faith in the life and work of Jesus Christ and by surrender of the same self-will that burdened Adam and Eve.

## 2. Redemption and Salvation

I believe and embrace all the claims of Jesus Christ: that he is the Son of God and God himself, one third of the Holy Trinity; that his birth was of the virgin mother Mary, his life was sinless and his death was a prophesied payment for the sins of mankind for all times. I believe that the historical resurrection of Christ from the grave paved a passageway into eternal life for all who seek God to the best of their knowledge and ability. He will, on the day of the Father's choosing, return to earth to judge the living and the dead; and those who have chosen repeatedly and ultimately to be separated from God by their sin and selfishness will be given their just desserts. I believe that the sacrificial blood of Jesus Christ is the most precious commodity ever to have touched the earth and is sufficient to bring salvation to all souls in Heaven and on earth for all time. As Christ said, "No one comes to the Father except through me" (John 14:6), therefore his work has created and opened the door for any and all who would enter into a relationship with God. Though some may be slow to identify Christ as the source of their salvation, he is nevertheless the Way, the Truth, and the Life for all who are saved from themselves and their sin, and who exhibit the fruit of the Spirit while living as citizens of the invisible realm of Heaven, even while at home on earth.

## 3. Transformation and Sanctification

I believe that the Holy Spirit, the Comforter promised by Jesus Christ, descended on the church on the Day of Pentecost and continues to indwell all believers with the intent of transforming them further into the likeness of God. This Spirit was poured out first on the apostles and later freely given to all Christ-believers who, in faith, made the decision to repent and turn from their sinful way of living and submitted to an immersion in water. In early church history and New Testament teaching, this act called baptism was more than a dipping or dunking of the body in water—it was also an inward washing and filling by the Holy Spirit. According to the apostle Paul's letter to the church at Ephesus, there was only one baptism (Ephesians 4:5), so this immersion in Spirit and water must have occurred via the same experience. In Romans 6, baptism is a means of identifying with the death and resurrection of Christ; we are buried with him through baptism in order to be raised with him in a new life. For the lifetime of the believer, this Spirit then ministers with a touch of divine sensitivity and is readily available to teach, comfort, encourage, and guide with a gentle hand those who seek God through his Word, nature, creativity, community, testimony, service, and silence. The process of sanctification, being transformed from the inside out, occurs on God's timetable, by God's power, and is primarily God's job. Our part in the progression of spiritual maturity is in placing ourselves in a position to be changed by following the leadings of his Spirit and, in obedience, adhering to the best of our ability to the teachings and example of Jesus Christ, his apostles, prophets, and saints.

## 4. Guidance and Inspiration

The Word of God is described in Hebrews 4:12 as being "living and active. Sharper than any double-edged sword, it penetrates even to dividing soul and spirit, joints and marrow; it judges the thoughts and attitudes of the heart." Chapter 1 of the Gospel of John records that "the Word was with God, and the Word was God." From these verses I understand that the books and letters that make up the book we call the Bible do not encompass all that is intended by the phrase *Word of God*. While I have long believed that Scripture is inspired by God and was supernaturally dictated through holy men and protected from significant change through centuries of historical transition, I do not believe that God confines his communication with man to what can be read from a Bible passage. Quakers believe that God continues to reveal himself through an inner leading or inner light—often called the still, small voice—that seekers are able to trust as his voice, particularly when it is listened to and shared in communal gatherings for worship. It is important to mention here that this Quaker belief is buffered by the declaration that God will never reveal any message that directly contradicts truth as revealed in Scripture. I like this perspective and have seen it work well, as it allows the disciple to become more Christocentric and less of a bibliophile, worshipping the Living Word rather than the written Word of God.

In my multiple decades of being a Christ-follower, many times taking extreme measures to experience all that God has to offer the modern believer, I have never personally seen a supernatural physical healing, heard an astounding prophetic message from a person, or spoken in an unknown tongue. While I have been healed of many things, none of them has been in the biblically instantaneous manner. I believe the Holy Spirit is alive and well in the church and her members, and while this Spirit may at times be squelched by our behavior or lack of faith, I am not one who has seen the need for or evidence of the supernatural outpourings that seemed to be a staple of first-century Christianity. From what I have seen, the Spirit of God makes available all the power, love, grace, peace, forgiveness, freedom, and joy we can handle when we seek his will and ways with whatever enthusiasm and exuberance we can muster. I for one am grateful that my salvation, usefulness, and happiness does not depend on what gifts, knowledge, or experience I may possess or utilize, but on the life, death, burial, resurrection, and ascension of the living Christ who makes all of my paths—even the doctrinal one—straight. It is not doctrine that makes us right with God, but Christ. He must be worshipped above all systems of belief, no matter how doctrinally pure they may be.

# ( 20 )

# THE BIG QUIET

### *where* CHRIST *does*
### *his* BEST WORK

The irony exists that a culture or a person not at home with aloneness and solitude soon becomes swamped in loneliness. A cosmic loneliness takes over the soul when the soul can no longer feel the intimacy of communion with the many beloveds who bless us daily—from stars twinkling to grasses growing, from animals staring to flowers beaming. It takes a sense of inner silence to begin to appreciate the love and revelation and caring that are all around us in the other-than-human world. Loneliness feeds on a lack of aloneness, a dulled sensibility to solitude.

**Matthew Fox**
*Creativity: Where the Divine and the Human Meet*

The grieving was in full swing. As was the custom of the day, hired wailers and musicians had been summoned to enhance the sorrowful mood. Singing the blues was a legitimate vocation in those days. As if paid by the tear, these professional mourners were hard at work stirring up the emotions of gathered friends and family and making everybody cry. Unable or unwilling to participate in the pre-funeral party, the father of the deceased child had left the wake and returned with the one man, purportedly a miracle worker, who claimed he could heal the sick and raise the dead. Seeing his faith, Christ had responded to this man's plea for help and had followed him home. Upon entering the house, Jesus immediately went to work—his first order of business, creating a climate of quiet wherein he could perform his miracle. The contracted noisemakers laughed at his seeming inability to distinguish between sleep and death, but they left without argument. "After the crowd had been put outside, he went in and took the girl by the hand, and she got up" (Matthew 9:25).

While Jesus naturally became the center of attention wherever he went because of his reputation for miracles and his appealing, though paradoxical, rhetoric, making a scene for the sake of show or spectacle was not his modus operandi. Never in Scripture do we read that Jesus intentionally created a moving or excitable atmosphere in order to heal someone or teach a lesson. His antagonists or the profiteers usually did enough of this, leaving him the job of quieting things down. No flashy tent revivals with neon crosses or frothy emotional appeals were necessary for the Son of God to do his work. On the contrary, Jesus preferred to calm stormy seas and pacify hungry bellies before tossing out his pearls of wisdom and life-changing truth. "Fear not," "Let not your hearts be troubled," and "Blessed are the peacemakers" were just some of the words spoken by Christ when the mood and crowd around him were anxious and amped up. Often ridiculed by the doubting religious right of his day, Jesus' earthly demise was likely accelerated (though all part of the plan) by his lack of interest in producing on-demand miracles or performing supernatural party tricks. For these were what an authentic messiah or prophet would do—if he were indeed the real thing—according to the educated scholars and teachers of the Old Covenant law. We would later hear them saying something like "If you are the Messiah as you say you are then come down (from the cross) and save yourself." Rather than creating a noisy fuss, Christ's primary intention was to communicate messages such as "The kingdom of God is within" and "Blessed are the meek." And this he shared through both his humble (though not weak) manner and his quiet (though not soft) words. This sacred space of silence, the Big Quiet, was the preferred platform of the king of the Jews.

The rooms of my heart and head must be cleared and quieted for Christ's work to have its best effect. When my conscious mind runs on like a hamster wheel at midnight, or noon for that matter, spinning with self-centered fear and squeaking with temporal desires, there is not much chance of my hearing or responding to the still, small voice within that comes from God. God loves me enough not to compete for my attention, but waits patiently within earshot until I am ready to receive the words of hope and direction he offers. While I believe God holds the formula for my heart's transformation and is solely responsible for my soul's sanctification, it is my job to put myself in the position each day whereby I can be reached beyond the noisy thoughts, feelings, concerns, and even wordy prayers that can crowd my busy, conniving mind. It is up to me to create and frequently visit the tranquil places where I can be available for God's handiwork.

Quieting the mind and spirit are skills that require training and effort to be effective. Closer to the truth, finding the Big Quiet and sitting comfortably with it is an inside job that in itself requires a spiritual awakening. Religious practitioners in Western society sometimes ridicule those who practice meditation—a sign of ignorance of the true value of this spiritual art. Unaware of or perhaps indifferent to their relationship to more than 1,500 years of Christian tradition developed, practiced, and guarded by Catholic brothers and sisters, Protestants fail to see their own heritage in contemplative expressions of worship and community. While frequently relegated to monks and nuns as part of their job training for sainthood, meditation or centering prayer is really a source for power and contentment that is available to any who strive to take the time to sit still and experience the presence of God in their own hearts.

Loud surroundings are not too difficult to find or create these days. What is disturbing to me, however, is how we are exposed to the same high decibel levels in our church gatherings as we are in traffic or in our daily marketplace transactions. There are modern versions of wailings galore, including bassy frequencies, ringing guitars, and overzealous song leaders. ("This time, sing it like you mean it!") Silence and stillness, precious and rare commodities to modern religious services, require courage and deliberate intention on the part of the worship leader. Those entrusted with planning meetings for worship must believe and commit themselves to the principle that God is already present in his people and does not need to be awakened from some distant sleeping place with loud music and high-energy crowd involvement.

God awaits our recognition of his perfect love, amply supplied in the heart of every believer who would acknowledge it. But he will not crash through the gates of our free will (or our orders of worship) to make us receive it. Our oldest and truest expression of worship, while also that of which modern Christians have the least experience, lies in reverently placing ourselves in a position to experience the corporate Big Quiet and to celebrate a deeper awareness of his presence in our gathering and in our lives. Moreover, this spiritual gift is available to every believer, every day, in every place—not only when we gather in unity as the body of Christ.

I can't figure out why having a more contemporary worship service means louder music and a busier format. Where did the assumption come from that spiritual outsiders or even insiders have such short attention spans that they need to be entertained in order to hear a message of God's grace, love, and power? When did the church lose its cultural distinction from a society that cannot sit still long enough to eat a meal, read a book, or share a simple conversation? Where have the congregations gone that practice a quiet "call to worship," the time traditionally reserved for meditation and prayer before the vocal formalities of a worship service begin? Thank goodness we still have the Quakers and the Trappist Monks to provide examples of sitting and waiting on God as paths to experiencing his touch. Little by little, however, Christians of all brands and doctrinal stances are embracing the call to the Big Quiet and returning to the balanced perspective of worship and faith that the church once enjoyed before it relegated the ways of meditation to the Eastern religions and the Western monasteries. If current trends continue, soon enough our worship gatherings, Bible studies, and prayer groups will all reflect the beauty and grace of this door of God, which Thomas Merton called The Palace of Nowhere. And in faith, if we meet him in the Big Quiet, Christ will appear and do his best work in and among us even if we appear to be dead or asleep.

# (21)

# SILENCE AND SOLITUDE

## MEAT *and* POTATOES *for the* SOUL

Let there always be quiet, dark churches in which men can take refuge. Places where they can kneel in silence. Houses of God, filled with his silent presence. There, even when they do not know how to pray, at least they can be still and breathe easily. Let there be a place somewhere in which you can breathe naturally, quietly, and not have to take your breaths in continuous short gasps. A place where your mind can be idle, and forget its concerns, descend into silence, and worship the Father in secret.

**Thomas Merton**
*New Seeds of Contemplation*

After two days of steady sandblasting from a brutal March nor'easter, the winter-to-spring winds have calmed and the horizontal rains, typical of the North Carolina barrier islands, have once again ceased. The severity of the storm has served to increase the intensity of the calm. Standing on the emerald coast at the top of a sea-oat-covered dune, I turn my neck in a half-moon sweep to see the nautical horizon stretch from three to nine o'clock. Save for a fishing vessel laboring a half-mile out and a Coast Guard plane passing overhead, I have the beach all to myself. The afternoon sun-ripened heat draws the scent of salty sweet marsh from the Pamlico mud banks, and southern winds swirl it up and around to mingle with the ocean mist. The smell is intense and intoxicating as it hits my face. I can taste the brine with my nose, and my spit is like saltwater.

Groups of killdeer and sandpipers, willets and terns jump up from their one-legged resting poses to comb the beach for dinner. Each wave deposits tiny courses of their meal, which they collect much as the storied Hebrews gathered their manna in the desert. With every foamy pass, their daily bread is provided by the God of sand and sea. Every once in a while, a laughing gull, misinterpreting the toss of a stone or piece of shell for an invitation to dinner, lets out a musical squawk that breaks the silence, causing me to realize I haven't heard a human voice, including my own, for quite some time.

Out in the remote, off-season beaches, forests, and mountain ranges, silence and solitude are not difficult to discover. In fact, it would take quite a bit of work to ignore them. They are waiting to be harvested by anyone willing to take a day or an hour to wade into the seaside vineyard or hike through the sage-covered canyons. Even in the countryside pasture or alfalfa field, the solitude can be so weighty you can feel it pressing in on you like some sort of g-force. Closer to home, these silent spaces for God touches can also be found in the shopping mall parking lot or the backyard lounge chair, when one stops the daily treadmill long enough to listen to the whispers of God. To the practiced contemplative, God is waiting to be heard in many varied experiences of daily life, quiet and otherwise, when time and care are taken to develop a regular pattern of spiritual listening. The soul-seeker who learns how to slow down, sit down, and do nothing but revel in the sanctity of the moment finds it possible, over time, to recreate this God-reaching occurrence in almost any place or circumstance. On the other hand, no amount of external hush can produce quietness of heart and soul if one is not interested in heeding the internal, passive voice of the Creator God. No amount of outer calm can silence the noises of the head or smooth the rough currents of the heart, where both real and imagined traffic jams.

My journey into silence and solitude has occurred in many ways and places over the years. Some days when living on the Carolina coast, it meant walking a sandy driveway two blocks to the Atlantic beach or riding my bicycle to the hurricane-weakened, pelican-populated fishing pier. When living full-time in a motor home, I found myself with the luxury of spending entire weeks in places like the deserts of Nevada, the Everglades of Florida, or the mountains of Tennessee, where lengthy conversation with anyone besides my quiet-loving wife was a rarity. These days, I most often encounter my silent solitude each morning at home in a well-worn, lime-green reading chair; a spiritual book and writing journal in my lap (often accompanied by a cat), and a hot cup of coffee on my paint-stained lamp table. This is the heart of my quiet kingdom, where I feel no pressure to think, feel, or say anything significant. Being in the present is good enough, and a simple awareness of this openness to God's input is my best expression of meditation.

Over the years, in these daily quiet times I have developed a practice of listening to God, rather than telling God things that may or may not matter in the long run. I have come to believe that, on any given day, I do not know what is necessary or best for others or me in this lifetime. Therefore, as best as I can, I attempt to settle down and practice the lost art of inner solitude, letting go of outer expectations and trying to get out of God's way. Twenty minutes of centering prayer in the morning and again in the afternoon can set me straight for a whole day of God-following. In addition, five minutes and a few deep breaths can do wonders for the flagging spirit and crowded head in the middle of the day. Whether walking or sitting, driving or working, playing or having a conversation, there is strength to be found in silence and wisdom, waiting to be mined from the golden veins of solitude.

There is a common assumption in church circles that God speaks most frequently and the clearest through singing worship and heart-enlivened sermons. Yet I find the context of speechless tranquility to be a more common ground for God-messaging than any activity with noise, no matter how holy the words. This is the "Be still" part of "Be still, and know that I am God" which goes on to say, "I will be exalted in the earth" (Psalm 46:10). According to the psalmist, God is praised in our practice of stillness and silence. Going even further, St. John of the Cross, a Spanish poet and mystic from the sixteenth century, said, "Silence is God's first language." From all I have read, heard, learned, and experienced about the God of the Bible and the same God of the universe, his greatest desire appears to be to share space and consciousness with his people through gift-giving, conversation, and friendship.

In this daily silence and solitude, wherever and however I experience it, I get a taste of my right and humble place on this planet and once more feel the swell of gratitude and sense of belonging that come from trusting God's will and way for my life. In these moments of stillness found in early morning walks, bicycle rides, or late-night prayers from the back porch, I am reminded that these sacred segments are precious and scarce in an increasingly busy and populated society. Silence is not the widened way of this world; it is a slender, rough-cut trail up the backside of the mountain that few dare to travel. It is part of the narrow path that Christ spoke of, a leg of the road less traveled that leads to the "Today is the day of salvation" kind of stuff, even for those who consider themselves already saved. In times of stillness, we are saved, not from sin or Hell, but from ourselves and all the petty worries, fears, and ego ideas that often have us running around like puppies chasing their short and insignificant tails. In this quiet salvation, God again becomes God of our lives and we are relieved of our need to compete with him for the universal throne.

Because of its otherworldly characteristics, over the centuries the mystical experience of individual and collective silence has been a regular practice and core value of the Christian community; a passageway into the divine present practiced daily by surrendered saints and sometimes even by everyday believers. Part of the lure of the monastic life has always been the opportunity for a deeper walk with God through the life of solitude that a cloistered society provides. I have yet to meet a spiritually-minded man who has not, at one time or another, fantasized about living the life of a priest or monk. While it is difficult to imagine living without some of the conveniences and luxuries to which we Americans have grown accustomed, the idea of having specific hours each day to read, pray, and tend to dumb animals while making wine, cheese, or candles has never lost its appeal. In modern times, the way of silence and solitude can be likened to the course of a salmon swimming upstream, going against the spiritual grain of a culture that lives and breathes accomplishment and the acquisition of material belongings. This way of stillness, not commonly found or talked about in twenty-first-century America, is not for everyone. It is, however, available to all those who are unwilling to wait for the ethereal mists of Heaven to get their hands on the keys to the kingdom. Silence and solitude are for those who desire to hear God speak and watch the Spirit move in the cracks and the spaces of life. Here and now.

It should come as no surprise to anyone new to the discipline of silence that it is not easy. One would not normally expect to be a great musician or athlete without practice (except for golfers who all expect to be good without working at it), so the same measure should apply here. While practice can sometimes make perfect, other times it simply makes practicing easier. For two years, I was gifted with an opportunity to live, work, and play among some evangelical Quakers in Oregon. While they were not as simple or removed from society as the Amish, the Quakers, also known as Friends, taught me much about shared silence and listening for the sense of the group. Until this exposure to Quaker worship, I had never sat in intentional silence without a good reason, except as punishment for pulling a girl's ponytail or for talking too much in class. Sure, I had many times when I was alone or with people and just not talking, but it was never with an intention of listening to what God might say to me in the moment. In my early experiences of unvoiced worship, I was pleasantly surprised to discover that shared silence was much easier to enjoy than any of my solo attempts had been. Most people understand the difficulty of quieting the mind in attempts at meditation or quiet reflection, and I was no exception. However, in a group of people all trying to connect at some level with Christ, the present teacher, there is a common energy in the shared silence that gives you a sense of your mind being weighted down. A group gravity of sorts helps your mind to stay focused and not wander so much. Once you experience this phenomenon, you find yourself wanting more—the fellowship with God and others becomes so accessible.

The search for solitude and silence with groups of God-believers is what drives my current, resurrected desire to rejoin the ranks of local church leadership. From all I am hearing, the church is hungry for more quiet and intimate worship experiences that can help add a sense of meaning and intimacy to their relationships with God and each other. There are also many outside the institutional church who are thirsty for fresh God experiences that can satisfy a deep, unexplained longing for something significant. Creative worship gatherings that emphasize prayer and meditation, and that "hold space" for uncomfortable but useful periods of stillness may quite possibly be a common ground on which newcomers to faith and seasoned churchgoers can meet for authentic God touches. At this point in my spiritual journey, having seen much of what isn't working and some of what works quite well for helping people to connect with God, I find myself unwilling to expend much of my energy doing what someone else can do or is already doing. I am putting all of my eggs in the spiritual baskets of silence and solitude with hopes that those inside and outside the structured church will develop a taste for the nourishment and satisfaction that these staples of spiritual growth can bring. Why settle for chips and salsa when meat and potatoes are waiting to be devoured? Dinner is served.

# ( 22 )

# CREATION

## *the* NATURE STORE
## *that* NEVER CLOSES

A philosopher asked Saint Anthony: "Father, how can you be enthusiastic when the comfort of books has been taken away from you?" And Anthony replied: "My book, O Philosopher, is the nature of created things, and whenever I want to read the word of God, it is right in front of me.

**Joan Chittister**
*Illuminated Life: Monastic Wisdom for Seekers of Light*

When the summer tourist season and autumn's fishing term finally fade into a winter stillness on Hatteras Island, there are fewer pod-loaded minivans and bike-toting diesel trucks to buzz past the roadside homes of the locals. What is typically a one-second gap between the motored-up, tire-whining swooshes of vehicles mercifully becomes one- to five-minute pauses by day and one-hour respites at night. Much to their relief, year-round residents—human and otherwise—can once again enjoy longer periods of silence to take in the ear-sweetening voices of nature. These sensorial outcries, springing up from rain-soaked grounds and floating down from sun-painted skies, are sirens of solitude, leading the open-minded wanderer down hidden passages to the gardens of God. In earnest, these sounds of joy shout to a world numb from material excesses and bone-tired from racing rats and call the sojourner to retreat, heed the beauty, and hear the poetry in the shadows of the roadside hush. Chatting cardinals, chirping thrush, croaking frogs, tapping woodpeckers, even chiding starlings bring music to the ears as they hop, scurry, flit, and fly among the trees and shrubs, singing of a Creator who is providing for us all, filling our hearts and bellies from an unfathomable source of love and nourishment. "Come, take the hand of nature, and dance to the rhythm of freedom," they cry. "Come and hear the silent roar of the sustenance of life." To those willing to stop, listen, and breathe in its goodness, the touch of God streams through nature to enhance the journey and enable the creation of a new day and a new existence.

On calm days at the Outer Banks when the ocean breeze is somewhat easterly, a constant crash of rogue waves can be heard climbing over sand dunes and gliding past shore houses, beckoning the beachcomber to walk, wade, and discover the fragile gifts left for the gathering at the end of a foamy tide line. This is the nature store that never closes and where everything is free, though not everything is alive. Today's special is delicate purple starfish, scattered along the shoreline by the dozen—like flower petals dropped from a child's basket at a chapel wedding. Purple is not the typical color of starfish that show up on the Atlantic seaboard, especially ones dotted on their topside with what a non-marine biologist could mistakenly identify as a bright orange eye. If it were an eye rather than some data port or exposed piece of central nervous system, it would be opened wide to observe the disappointing destiny of being stranded high and dry for ghost crabs to forage into food, and for man to gather into soon-to-be-discarded shell collections. There is sadness in the fate of this blue-violet invertebrate, but beauty in the acceptance of its inevitable lot. Once out of water, starfish—like jellyfish and mollusks—have no method of navigating their way back to safety. They are victims of the very sea that once gave them life.

Lying helpless and hard, slightly pungent in odor, only hours after being deposited powerless on dry sand, these purple fallen stars serve as a reminder of my daily dependence upon the tides and times of God, much of which is not understood until seen clearly through the rearview mirror of retrospect. Faith is the invisible commodity that enables us to let go of limited understanding in exchange for the power to do the next right thing, the grace to learn from our less-than-best choices, and the wisdom, in time, to know the difference. No one or thing has as much power to live or die as he thinks he does. It is a trust march for all beings that walk upright. The animal and plant kingdoms, unblessed (or should I say uncursed?) with rational minds, rely upon God without question. It is wired into their

DNA to do God's will. On the contrary, those of us who make up the "intelligent species" seem quite content to accept the universal principles of relying on deity the hard way: We don't do it until we are convinced it has become absolutely necessary. Unaware that we are swallowing hook, line, and sinker the fish story that property and prosperity have some kind of power to save us from ourselves, we are expending much of our energy in pursuit of the stuff that virtually severs the spiritual connection we have to God and each other. We are caught by the gills in the nets of marketing campaigns that sell us a false sense of security in houses, clothes, cars, and all the accessories for these that cash and credit can buy. Temporary things that rain can rust, moth can eat, and that man can break in and steal are blocking us from our deep-seated need to trust and follow paths of spirit and truth. These are our only reliable sources of contentment and eternal gain. We are all starfish stranded on the beach, watching our destinies unfold. Only the spiritually destitute among us are blessed enough to have an orange eye open—ready to see the good that God wants.

There is great hope in this supernatural way of naturally being touched by God, especially for the spiritually hungry but religiously weary traveler. This means that, since God may be found and experienced anywhere at anytime, there is no mandate or pressure to attend certain services or say particular phrases to invoke God's presence or seek God's help. Because of the work of Christ, the God of the universe who answers to many names and works in untold ways is fully prepared to embrace any and all who would seek him with an open and sincere heart. There is no way to tell where this point of origin, this launch of faith, will take you, for world history is filled with altruistic humanitarian causes and perpetuating spiritual movements that began with one single-hearted believer who simply became willing to throw caution to the wind for the chance to love God and serve others. True faith will eventually lead the follower into experiences of sacrifice and progressive commitment, but not without the rewards of joy and a deep sense of meaning and purpose. This journey continues into a world without end, but begins one day at a time with a regular conscious focus on living out the ways of God.

With loud voices we cry in unison, "Where will we find it?" and "How will we know we have it?" These are good queries, but the more important questions are likely to be "What are we willing to do to seek it?" and "How willing are we to give it away in order to keep it?" From my experience, we most often truly see, feel, taste, hear, and experience God on the simple courses in life, the ordinary paths that lead to intersections with the extraordinary. And if one is as privileged as Francis of Assisi was to have an ear tuned to the voice of God in creation, this just might begin and end with the beauty of a flower or the song of a bird, the warmth of the sun, and the glow from the moon. Fortunately, for those willing to go God shopping regularly in the great outdoors, the creation store never closes and all God touches are free for the asking.

# ( 23 )

# DEATH

## HIGHWAYS, HALLOWEEN, *and* HARI-KARI

If we have a side that is fearful of life and attracted to death, it would help explain why our world seems so dominated by death and its agents. Why do we go so easily to war, even in an age when doomsday weapons could destroy all life? Why are we drawn to "entertainment" that involves depictions of violence and killing? Why do we so readily embrace the notion that there are "acceptable levels of death" from carcinogenic chemicals and nuclear power plants? Perhaps because we are afraid of life, of its challenges and demands for change. Perhaps because we perversely prefer the safe and predictable confines of the grave.

**Parker J. Palmer**
*The Active Life: Wisdom for Work, Creativity, and Caring*

It is Easter and I am inundated with thoughts of death. I didn't get much sleep last night and have been tired and troubled all day long. Being raised religious, Good Friday was always the day reserved for remembering death and eating fish, while Easter was about looking forward to candy and resurrections. Halloween, my favorite childhood holiday, holds the dark distinction of being about both death and candy. Nothing seems hopeful or sweet today, however, at least not in my village. Last night, shortly after midnight, four people riding bicycles and skateboards were run over by a distracted driver just a few blocks from my front door. Two of them were killed. Rousted out of bed by the flashing lights and sirens, I stumbled outside only to be suddenly exposed to the alarming details of a fatal accident. One victim, a woman of twenty-five years, was lying in the road covered by a blue tarp, and a twenty-six-year-old man lay dead in the ambulance; a nearby ditch filled with his blood and evidence of the medics' struggle to save his life. Two crushed bicycles, one broken skateboard, and several shoes were scattered along the roadside shoulder. Handfuls of residents gathered at the scene and were all standing in disbelief as police officers milled about, looking for witnesses and spray-painting outlines around evidence and debris. Someone said he saw the green Suburban veer off the road and smash into the unsuspecting pedestrians. I overheard another man, first on the scene after the accident, repeatedly describing the horror of scattered bodies and screaming survivors, as if his telling of the story might somehow make it not true.

Several people who knew the local driver were saying that he has a history of speeding tickets and drunk driving, but he has not yet been charged with any crime. I felt empathy for this man as he sat in the front seat of the state police cruiser, an overhead light illuminating his face for all passersby to see. He stared straight ahead as if patiently waiting for a very bad movie to end—in shock from the trauma of the death he had caused. Only time will tell how his life will be permanently imprinted by the consequences of one split-second lapse in attention, one fateful reach for a ringing cell phone.

In moments like these, death seems especially harsh, highlighting the mortal curse cast upon all of humanity by the first disobedient couple in the magical, mystical Garden of Eden. *Whom can we blame for these deaths that, by all appearances, were simply a matter of mathematically improbable and unfortunate timing? What is the point of getting up for a sunrise service on Easter morning when skies are gray and showers are impending? Where is the light at the end of the empty tomb? How much rain will it take to clear the blood from the highway?* These are only some of the questions rattling around in my head as I attempt to fall asleep. When I walked in the door after loitering at the scene of the accident last night, my wife said she could sense death on me. I could feel it too, and am having trouble shaking loose from this uncomfortable shroud. Like everything else in the realm of spirit, overcoming these circumstances and their effects will require faith in unseen power, mercy, justice, and love. Without something beyond our own understanding to trust and believe in, we face the prospects of insane thinking and dark decisions. This is an extreme example of finding life on life's terms to be unacceptable, but a perfect opportunity to embrace the notion that God has reasons for everything under the sun. I don't have to know what those reasons are, but if I intend to find peace in all situations, I do have to accept that everything is a piece of God's grand puzzle that I cannot see from my earthbound perspective.

In this regard, even dying can be an opportunity to see with a God's-eye view. For those who happen to be the ones doing the dying, death is an interstate highway with an HOV (high occupancy vehicle) lane to eternity, with no rest stop for making a deathbed confession. But for those of us with another day to live on this planet in these temporal skins, dying can also mean a path of faith to God. Many believe this is possible because of the self-fulfilling prophetic death and resurrection of Jesus Christ, some two thousand years ago. According to Old Testament tradition, a messiah would come from a chosen lineage and fulfill the Hebrew law by becoming the perfect sacrifice for the sins of all mankind. This work, which would unify all God-believers into one spiritual nation, would be completed by the miraculous life, brutal crucifixion, and triumphant resurrection of the Lamb of God. So far, at this point in our history, Jesus of Nazareth is the only one to have claimed to be that Messiah, led that life, died that death, and risen from that grave. Unlike all other spiritual leaders and teachers, Christ has no grave to which pilgrimages are made. History also attests to the fact that, while Christianity (as with all world religions) has perpetually been racked and recognized by human flaws and errors, millions of lives have been and continue to be transformed by faith in and obedience to Christ.

Though it is obvious not all worshippers agree on the name or dogma for God, it is possible that the life and work of Jesus Christ was so profound, so all encompassing that it has opened doors of salvation for all who would seek God with a faith and practice as honest and sincere as they can muster (as said in Hebrews 11:6 "anyone who comes to him must believe that he exists and that he rewards those who earnestly seek him"). This authentic faith leads to the dying of self with all its motives, desires, and designs. Eternal life is no longer considered a quantity of existence beyond the grave but a quality of life in the here and now that is other-centered and always growing. Once we begin to participate fully in the life (and death) cycles that God has ordained for planet, plant, people, and even pests, we no longer look at dying through the same eyes. Dying to self, thanks to the death and resurrection of Christ, leads to life that is ultimately not affected by the first breaths and last gasps of our journey through this world. We have been changed and for the better.

Two of my favorite artists died in October of 2002. Elliott Smith (of *Good Will Hunting* and *The Royal Tenenbaums* soundtrack fame) apparently stabbed himself to death, Hari-Kari style, ending his bout with alcoholism, addiction, and depression. Mike Yaconelli (known for his radical Christian periodical, *The Wittenburg Door*, and his book *Messy Spirituality*) was killed in a one-vehicle crash traveling south along I-5 from Medford, Oregon. His family was following a few minutes behind him in another vehicle and arrived at the scene after he had died. It was later discovered that Mike had died from a heart attack before the car had even come to a complete stop.

These two creative men, sold out to living their muse and leading lives of humble and immeasurable creative impact, influenced both my spiritual and career paths, though neither one knew it. Yaconelli gave me hope for the church and youth ministry over three decades simply by being willing to say what many of us were thinking but were afraid to admit. He helped me to see that I was always going to be screwed up and that God was OK with that—in fact, he loved me just as I was. Smith showed me through his melancholy tunes and lyrics that it is acceptable to sing about everyday life in the same language that you speak it, and that honesty is a high-rise apartment with many floors. His songs (see www.SweetAdeline. net) and Jon Krakauer's *Into the Wild*, the memoir of a society and reality dropout, have helped me as much as anything to embrace the significance of writing about the details of my average, though interesting, life.

Only the grace of God knows the wheres, whos, whats, and whens of Heaven, but I am enjoying the thought that the youth ministry guru and the suicidal mope-rocker might have met for the first time on All Hallows Eve while standing in line outside the pearly gates. Regarding his life on earth, Mike would have probably said, "Wow, man. What a ride!" only to hear Elliott's response, "I'm glad that's finally frickin' over!" Then much to their surprise, Jesus himself might have answered the door with, "You kids look soooo cute! Now, what do you say?" To which the two men, draped in their new heavenly bodies and dapper eternal garb would have replied in unison, "Trick or treat, smell my feet, give us something good to eat!"

The problem with death is that we, the remnant living, view it with such horror and finality that we are consumed by our own selfish grief and fail to see the new beginning ahead for those who have passed into the next dimension of reality. Thanks to the unfathomable life, murder, resurrection, and ascension of Jesus Christ, death—for those willing to carry a minuscule amount of faith around in this life—is a door that opens to freedom, peace, and understanding. I won't really get it myself until I take that last breath and wonder on the way out, "Will anyone pay attention to my music, writing, or art now that I'm gone?"

It's probably not unusual that I have been thinking about death since I was born. But like most folks I know, I avoid at all costs the thought of those close to me dying. I am not prepared to deal with death, and I have recently realized that nothing in our culture has helped me to get ready for this very common experience. All other cultures do; we've just eliminated it in the West. With all the flak that Halloween gets for its celebration of all things dead, wouldn't it be ironic if God has given us this time of year to remind us that life as we know it is temporary and all we really have is today? Death is just another mile on the Greyhound bus of this ethereal, eternal life. Good-bye Elliott, Mike, and the bicyclers on NC-12. I hope to see you soon. Save me a seat by the window and be prepared to share your Halloween candy.

# (24)

# FRIENDSHIP

## *a* SUPERHERO
## FAITH

> And a youth said, Speak to us of Friendship. And he answered, saying: Your friend is your needs answered. He is your field which you sow with love and reap with thanksgiving. And he is your board and your fireside. For you come to him with your hunger, and you seek him for peace.
>
> **Kahlil Gibran**
> *The Prophet*

I have a friend who gets a bad haircut every year so he won't be tempted to take a high-paying corporate job. He doesn't care whether his socks match. He doesn't own a TV, a computer, or a cell phone, but somehow stays abreast of world events and in touch with friends from around the globe. By all appearances, Ethan Hughes is a grown man, though he often masquerades as a superhero character that resembles a composite of Underdog and Dudley Do-Right, performing acts of service for any and all who ask. Choosing to take only the most basic public transportation, Ethan, also known to his superhero allies as "Blazin' Echidna," hasn't driven or ridden in a car or airplane since 1996. As a result, bicycling has become a way of life for him. The Eugene, Oregon, public transit drivers who watch him load his bike on the front of the bus each day know him as much by the hand-painted "Peace" on his helmet as by his name.

Having abandoned a successful career in marine biology, Ethan recently taught at a Quaker high school and intentionally lives on less than eight thousand dollars a year to avoid paying taxes that would go toward supporting the American war industry. A few years back, he gave away a sizable inheritance in order to explore more freely a life of simplicity and trust in God and the people he believes God puts in his path. Ethan and some of his eco-friendly comrades live in a small Earth-loving, organic-farming, compost-toilet-using community and eat mostly what they can produce in partnership with nature. These hyper-natural people are committed to treading lightly upon the planet, so they joyfully avoid conspicuous consumption and recycle religiously. When I last visited the Echo Hollow community, they were working on converting their common car, an old diesel Mercedes, to run on used cooking oil. In time, they hope to fuel up for free at grease traps behind fast-food restaurants.

I am grateful for the positive impact these friends have had on my life, though I have yet to figure out how to live out the new ecologically aware consciousness they have helped to awaken in me. If I ever get the chance some day, I would relish the opportunity to live in community with like-minded Spirit-seekers and grow organic food, fertilized by a compost pile, next to a pen of chickens roaming in a fruit orchard watered by a mountain stream.

I first met Ethan and his cohorts at a "Prayers for Peace" rally in 2002, which he organized in an effort to affect America's plans to invade Iraq. (I can still feel the sense of powerlessness we all felt as our governmental leaders were making a case for war that didn't sound logical to many of us outside the TV-hypnotized, media-drunk culture.) Everyone present that day was given the opportunity to read or say the prayer of his or her choice, and a silent reflection was observed between each one. While none of the local evangelical pastors chose to attend, though all were invited, many of the readings that day were from the teachings of Christ and the prayers of some of those touched by his life, notably Francis of Assisi, Mother Teresa of Calcutta, and Mahatma Gandhi. I painted watercolors in my journal and read aloud from the Sermon on the Mount, surrounded by a surprising number of non-Christians interested in Christ.

Early in the spring of 2003, as the White House war drums were getting louder and international peace protests were occurring more frequently, my friend Ethan decided it was time for drastic measures and made plans to sit for a month-long vow of silence and prayer. Before retreating to his shanty in the woods, he invited all those who desired to join him as often as they wished. Intrigued and curious, I wandered up the mountain on three or four different occasions to sit in silence with Ethan and others under the canopy of Douglas firs that towered above the moss-covered forest floor. High up in the Cascade foothills, there was little to hear but the light pelting of showers on the tin roof and the songs of wood birds living in harmony far from the violent sounds of gunfire and explosions. In retrospect, I would have visited and prayed with Ethan more often had I known how my life would be shaped by the few hours I spent listening to God and sharing space, love, and breath with this superhero friend.

Though Ethan is not comfortable with some of the trappings associated with the word *Christian*, I have met few people in my lifetime who more clearly showed me Christ in how they lived. In my fundamentalist upbringing, I was taught that it was always best if I chose Christians to be my friends—particularly ones who thought and believed the same as we did. People who were not Christians were considered a source of bad influence and if I was not careful, they would drag me straight down to Hell with them. The only good purpose of friendships outside the church was to "win people to Christ." This meant in part that I had to be prepared to convince them of their need for Jesus, be ready at all times to answer all their objections, and ignore any of their opinions and experiences with God as they had come to know him. This was called "friendship evangelism," though I don't recall making many friends this way. On the rare occasion that I did spark a friendship with a "nonbeliever" (or a Christian of a different variety, such as a Catholic), I often ran them off with my self-righteous attitude or scared them away with Christianese language, rather than enjoying the opportunity to see Christ in them or to simply love them as one of God's fellow creatures.

Since being touched by my friendship with Ethan, I have come to meet other people trudging a God path, albeit slow in their going, who are in the process of discovering that Christ has made the way for them, but who have yet to use these specific words to describe their experience. I now believe that it is presumptuous of me to assume that I can determine the spiritual condition and eternal destination of someone I meet simply by the words they use or the churches they don't attend. After all, Jesus himself said that by our fruit we would be recognized. Our love for others, particularly those outside the fold, demonstrates how we really feel about him. These days whenever I encounter friends in this world who are following the voice of God as best as they know how, whether they are card-carrying Christians or not, I am careful not to make any judgments about what they might need to know or do in their spiritual lives. For all I know, God may be using them to convert me.

# ( 25 )

# A LOOSE GRIP

## HEARING GOD *and*
## HELPING PEOPLE

Our book is meant to be suggestive only. We realize we know only a little. God will constantly disclose more to you and to us. Ask him in your morning meditation what you can do each day for the man who is still sick. The answers will come, if your own house is in order. But obviously you cannot transmit something you haven't got. See to it that your relationship with him is right, and great events will come to pass for you and countless others. This is the Great Fact for us.

*Alcoholics Anonymous*

One of the men in the golf club I used to play at had a bumper sticker on his golf cart that read, "Do I *look* like I give a @!+$?" People who knew him said this bumper sticker suited him like the name Buzz would suit a barber. While I'm not sure how well this slogan worked for the guy at home with his wife or at work with his boss, it must certainly have taken some pressure off his golf game, especially after missed shots, when his turf divot flew farther than his ball, or when he duck-hooked a three-wood into the lake. Regardless of how this guy played golf, I heard God speak to me through his golf cart whenever I saw it driving away from the first tee. Sort of like the amiable and persistent freeway sign that spoke to Steve Martin's character in the movie *L.A. Story*. Only he could see and hear it, and it gave him important messages like, "The weather will change your life." From my experience, you have to pay attention to messages and messengers like these.

Although I do not hear God speak to me through every bumper sticker, and I am still sorting through the profundity of hearing God's voice in this manner, a few things have become clear to me. For one thing, I believe God wants me to keep a loose grip on life and not take myself and my impact on the residents of this planet so seriously. For those of us who believe that having a loose grip is not a bad thing, it is obvious that neither is it an easy thing. John Daly, the oft-troubled long-ball hitter, once signed my *Golf Digest* magazine with his motto, "Dan, Grip it and Rip it." Now, I have tried out this philosophy both on the tee box and in my approach to life and have discovered that, in spite of my best efforts, this wisdom was apparently not intended for amateurs such as me. Moreover, while my golf game has definitely benefited from a firm grip and an even tempo, God is teaching me through regular sightings of humanness and odd everyday stuff to keep my grip on life loose and my touch on people light. The older I get, the more I am prone to believe the wise old woman who once told me that if I trust God with my life, then what happens next is none of my business. This should include my view of other people's lives as well.

As a young ministerial student in Bible college I chose Galatians 6:2, "Carry each other's burdens," as the text for my sermon in a preaching contest. I remember using the illustration of a tugboat pushing a barge up the Ohio River, exclaiming with equal ignorance and force our responsibility as mature believers to carry the burdens of those unable to take responsibility for their own souls. I would not-too-soon discover the fallacy of this belief and, after much pain and personal failure, find out that everyone is indeed responsible for his or her own life and growth—including me. Not that I have ever really carried anyone or their burdens, I have been way too self-centered for that. However, I have certainly suffered from the delusion of caring enough to try. Rather than making much of a difference, I have been like the guy holding a leg of a piano that is getting hauled up a flight of stairs by five other people. I have never really carried that much weight, but acting as if I have has somehow made me feel better about myself.

In my current dealings with people, I frequently find myself willing to maintain a loose grip for the sake of preserving my own health and happiness and to release others to do what they need to achieve the same. I recently told a friend that one of my strengths is my apparent ability not to be liked by everyone in order to be true to myself and helpful to others. I have figured out that not everyone

I have the privilege of helping is going to like me. Many people in Alcoholics Anonymous with long-term sobriety share a similar story of having a first sponsor whom they didn't like very much but who nevertheless helped save their lives. This may be true of anyone who uses a spiritual director or mentor as well. Who wants to be told what to do—even if it is for our own good and we happen to be asking for it? As long as my safety and sanity are not in jeopardy, whatever the people around me decide to do is not my concern, even though I may care about them deeply. The question is, "To what lengths are these people willing to go in order to live a surrendered life and take responsibility for their own actions?"

As many of us discover every day, much to our dismay, the world is full of people who don't want to turn the reigns of their lives over to the care of God, and who are content to grind out their daily existence with only wisps of happiness and glimpses of inner peace. It is entirely possible to cover up, albeit temporarily, a lot of spiritual sickness and self-will-run-riot with money, sex, drugs, work, and even religion. And it takes a lot of grace and courage to allow people to live life as they think it suits them, even if we can see better from our chairs. More than once I have been given just enough rope to hang myself by people who cared enough to let me go and watch me try to outrun myself. This inevitable mercy hanging helped bring my emotional bottom up to me where I could reach it in order to hand it over to God. For all I know, there are people in my life who are still handing me rope. Surrender of soul and wit are daily disciplines, not vacation destinations. And as I attempt to practice a loose grip these days on people in my life, I am aware that when I hand them yards of hemp and twine, this may appear as if I don't give a @!+$. Fact is, I do care. I just can only carry so many clubs in my bag.

My favorite golf story occurred a few years ago while I was playing a round at a Virginia Beach course called Hell's Point. One of my partners was an old friend who also happened to be my dentist, Dr. Thom Parrott. Late in the round, I hit a good drive and a great second shot on a par four and found myself putting for birdie. As I lined up to putt, I noticed something moving behind me. I turned to see a rooster, a Rhode Island Red, strutting across the green. Where he came from and where he was going remain, to this day, a mystery. All I know is that, at that moment, I was putting for birdie with a friend named Parrott while a big, red chicken was crossing the green to get to the other side. I was in the Bermuda Triangle of golf. Obviously, I cared about my situation, but I was not in control of the outcome.

As any golfer will tell you, there are times when bigger forces are at play in this gentlemen's game than mere men, the swings they take, and the lies they tell. There are gods of golf that get nodded to, prayed for, and cursed at who have never revealed why heavenly favor is shown to some hackers and denied others. Jokes are made about God's interest in golf, such as "When in a thunderstorm, to avoid being struck with lightning, hold up a one-iron, because even God can't hit a one-iron." But every serious golfer knows that St Andrews, Scotland—the birthplace of golf—is holy ground. Every golfer knows what perfection feels like in that rare (for most) moment when the club picks the ball from the bent grass without any indication of contact and sends it sailing skyward in an upward trajectory that lasts forever, only to see it stop in midair for a split-second before dropping within inches of the intended target, as if someone had walked up and placed it there by hand. Golf, in moments like these, holds a glimpse into the miraculous and is the reason men will pay any price for a piece of equipment if they believe it will help them to recreate that moment when they felt the touch of divinity in their hands and on their game.

The moment of my birdie/Parrott/rooster putt was another of those occasions where God had his hand and sense of humor in play and all was well, even if there was no explanation available for the mortals present. It is not a stretch to say that this is how God touches the lives of those who happen to be around me when the miracle of transformation occurs. While it may appear that my swing, posture, stance, or ability to concentrate had something to do with the perfect God shot, chances are it was simply God showing up because he felt like being a rooster or a parrot and he wanted to remind me that God can show up wherever and whenever and speak through whatever means God chooses. Even if that happens to be in the Bermuda Triangle or on a bumper sticker.

# (26)

# DISCOVERY

## SMILING DOGS *and* DANCING BIRDS

Remember thy Creator in the days of thy youth. Rise free from care before the dawn and seek adventures.

**Henry David Thoreau**
*Walden*

This morning I step sleepily from my warm cottage and into a face-full of bright sun. The abundance of azure headroom helps to clear my mind. "So, this is where you've been keeping all the sky," I say aloud as I button my jacket up to the top. With the temperature a crisp 28 degrees Fahrenheit, the wintry salt air forces me to pick up the typical pace of my daily stroll. At the end of my street, where the cracked asphalt curves into sand dunes, I take a right instead of my usual left and walk an extra block before cutting over to the beach. Stealing through a yard I've never set foot in before, I catch some subtle movement out of the corner of my eye and turn to see the face of a brown-and-white Boxer spying at me from around his private corner. I am not sure, but I could swear the corners of his mouth are turned up as if he is smiling. I stop for a moment to consider that he might very well be smirking at me, as if he was up to something sneaky like that cartoon dog, Muttley. Though he appears to have no interest in enforcing the No Trespassing sign I have chosen to ignore, I sense that he wants me to know that he could make my day a lousy one if he were so inclined. Guessing that this dog is more Petey (from the *Little Rascals*) than Kujo in temperament, I nevertheless give him the benefit of the doubt and quickly skip past the boundaries of his protected domain.

Out on the beach, I pick up a wave-weathered branch and walk along the high-tide line, flipping over pieces of shell in search of an addition for my collection. *One can never have too many sea shells*, I think to myself, *especially perfect ones*. My growing pile of conch and whelk shells back home reflect the frequency of these waterside walks of mine. A calf-high drift log calls my name, so I stop to sit for a while and let the sounds of wind and waves wash over me. The mid-morning sun soaks my exposed skin with love and vitamin D, and I feel cradled by its warmth. With great relief I let go of my fears and concerns and watch as they are carried out to sea on the backs of the porpoises and in the arms of Poseidon. There is no time, only now. No place, only here. This is God's living room, and the welcome mat is definitely out.

Overhead, circling upward in a thermal draft, are two large local birds, a sea gull and a pelican. Like yin and yang, they effortlessly dance opposite one another, unlikely partners in an East Coast version of *West Side Story*. What would prompt this improbable association? What is the attraction between these forbidden lovers? I can only guess they have been caught in some heavenly vortex, if not a wind shear—mere observers of their own reality, powerless over the forces at play in their ethereal ballet. Then suddenly, as if waking from a hypnotic trance, seemingly embarrassed by their discovered tryst, the gull and pelican spin away from one another and drift off in opposite directions as if they had never met. A once-in-a-lifetime thing. A-one-in-a-million encounter. Now over but never-ending. A stunning display of the handiwork of God.

Who could ever predict or manufacture such a magical meeting as this one? Not even the wealthiest man or woman could buy a ticket or reserve a seat to this effervescent opera. Premium events such as this are pure and unmistakable God shots that come only to those willing to make and hold space in their lives for such surprises and sideshows of the eternal. No matter where I happen to live, I have found that every day holds the promise of venture and discovery, available in simple, planned, or spontaneous jaunts into the wild. This defined but uncharted path to God leads us in search of things never before seen, uncovering clues and detecting evidence of the omnipresent touch. This unearthing of fresh experience is inevitably available to anyone willing to take the time to look, listen, and lean into the newness of each day.

At an earlier point in time, I once identified "time alone with God" exclusively as sitting alone with my Bible and journal, meditating on the meaning of certain Scriptures and praying for God's will in my life. These days I consider this daily quiet time but one way to experience and enjoy the presence of God. And while I religiously practice variations (mostly in the type of book I read) on this theme, I also count long walks in the woods, oceanside sauntering, and meaningful meanderings through my neighborhood as significant pieces to my passage of discovery. I don't mind the stereotypical criticisms that come my way when I am vocal about these soul touches, mostly New Age in their reference, for I truly believe that the hand of God grazes me in the cottonwood and aspen leaves that fall on the path before me. In the wood fires that swirl their smoke from sleepy chimneys and in the damp floor of the forest I can smell the Creator God at work. Under each upturned shell and in the smile of every dog hides the obtainable face of God, waiting to be discovered in both the ordinary and the extraordinary.

# (27)

# GOD

## JOLLY GIANTS
## *or* GROUPS *of* DRUNKS

In my opinion, there are two essential problems with believing God is something he isn't. The first problem is that it wrecks your life, and the second is that it makes God look like an idiot.

**Donald Miller**
*Searching for God Knows What*

S ome of my earliest thoughts about God were somewhat typical for a kid. In my mind, God was the jolly white giant (the good brother to both the jolly green giant and the bad "fee-fi-fo-fum" giant in *Jack and the Beanstalk*) who wore a long robe and beard and had really big feet. My guess is that my three-giants theory is what I came up with to understand the whole three-Gods-in-one Trinity thing. Try as I could not to be afraid of God, it was hard to get past the condemning images of the vengeful punisher I heard about most Sundays. At the time, I thought Wrath was God's middle name. As I was still confused by the difference between abstract and concrete thoughts, when adults talked about God in big-people terms, I could only imagine him in little-people pictures. For instance, the word *love* for me conjured up images of getting lots of Christmas presents and candy, while the word *judgment* meant spankings and being banished to my room while everyone else watched *Bonanza* or *The Dick Van Dyke Show*. In theory, I was expected to integrate the idea of a loving God—which was the one that good kids and generous adults got to see—with the judging God—who had it in for the mean kids and stingy adults. What with the number of adults I meet these days who are confused about God and what to believe about him, apparently I was not the only who didn't get the God things explained to him very clearly.

An increasing number of people share the historical, though unconventional, idea and practice that church is more about who they are and how they live than some building they visit on Sundays. Tired or bored with traditional methods of seeking God, many people (young adults in particular) are staying away from the institutional church and deciding instead to gather with friends and acquaintances on their own terms and turf so that they don't have to wade through all the religious details in order to talk about and to God. While congregations in tune with religious trends—the latest currently labeled the "emergent church"—have expended a lot of time and energy in attempting to program services attractive to these spiritual outsiders, most members of this target audience have already decided that their view of God is too big for any one place of worship. (God must certainly be bigger than all the giants, jolly green and otherwise, right?) Thus, as has always been the case since the first century, there is a church occurring under the radar but in the mix, meeting in hamlets, homes, and havens, whose numbers are not being recorded for weekly church attendance figures. Most ministers I know, however, would find a way to count them if they only knew where they were meeting.

There is another segment of the American population that also does not see the need for an organized church experience or want anyone dictating to them what they must believe in order to be blessed, loved, or saved by God. These people are members of an ever-growing population of anonymous and autonomous 12-step fellowships. Spiritually discouraged and religiously frustrated, in addition to dying from their disease, a majority of these alcoholics and addicts had all but given up on God because they believed they had tried God and found him lacking. But built into the program of Alcoholics Anonymous, some would say through divine inspiration, is a life-saving principle that has helped millions of agnostic and atheistic alcoholics to come to faith over the past seventy years—this is the idea of choosing your own conception of God, as you understand him, or higher power, if you will. Contrary to the concerns and objections of many Christians, the practice of this principle does not mean that 12-steppers fashion a fictitious or false god from their imaginations that conveniently works for them as they wish, like some sort of genie in a bottle. Nor do they automatically identify with someone else's idea of God (from Judaism, Buddhism, Hinduism, or even Christianity) just because it happens to be different from the one they had but couldn't get to work on their drinking and drugging problem. Rather, it is by broadening and at the same time simplifying their ideas of who or what God is that they find an effective way to accept spiritual help and direction and receive miraculous relief from the addiction that has been patiently and systematically killing them. (In the beginning some can only swallow the idea of God as standing for Good Orderly Direction or Group Of Drunks.) This place of faith, rather than being where they end up in their ideas of God, instead allows them a point of beginning—a jumping off place that would be otherwise out of reach if they were forced to comply with the tenets of a religion or a certain set of beliefs.

To those who have never been in a position to experience it, let me just say that allowing God to reveal himself to you, as he is and as he chooses, can prove to be a very freeing experience. While the idea of going beyond the limited viewpoints of God taught to us in Sunday school or through our parents' lifestyles can be quite scary, it can also allow God to show us something about who he is that perhaps we did not know. Imagine what we might learn or experience if we truly allow for the idea that there are things we do not know about God. If God is God, then our human capacity to comprehend him will always be confined to our limited understanding and perceptions, no matter how much we read or study the Bible. From what I have seen, it is not as important what we call God or what we believe about God as it is that we are open to the truth, freedom, and love that he can bring about in our lives when we seek him with an open heart, mind, and spirit. How we express our faith in words (theology, epistemology, ecclesiology, and etcetera-ology) is not nearly as important as how we prepare our hearts to receive it and to live it out in all our affairs. Jesus was pretty clear about this.

Like many before me, I had to quit my traditional church experience altogether before I could stumble into a more simple and meaningful way of relating to God. What has been surprising about this journey is that since peacefully disassociating myself from the church of my youth and young adulthood (leaving behind much of my own worthless bitterness and judgment), I have discovered that I am quite as much a part of the church that I grew up hearing about but never knew where to find. This church is nothing less than the union of Christ-centered beings who believe that people are more important than material possessions, that time well spent is more significant than hard-earned money, that conspicuous consumption is a poor substitute for spiritual poverty, and that the joy of creativity conjoins us to the Siamese soul of our Creator. This church is the fellowship of all believers who are willing to follow the mandates and mores, the direction and dictates of a personal supreme being (often referred to as God) as he chooses to reveal himself one day at a time. There are no impossible laws to obey or complicated ideas to understand, only a pure acceptance and practice of the truths common to many world religions: love God and serve others. The path to this relationship with God is littered with much letting go of old ideas and showered with the blossoms and blooms of new freedom and fresh grace. There are millions of believers traversing this sea of faith, many of whom do not know or see it, but who nonetheless, because of Christ, are experiencing the bon voyage. Some of us are even daring to enjoy the ride.

Interesting to some of my Christian friends but disturbing to others is my belief that there are innumerable souls (Muslims and Buddhists, Christian Scientists and Mormons, pagans and witches, agnostics and atheists) who are likely benefiting from the miraculous life, atoning death, saving resurrection, and bodily ascension of Jesus Christ, but who do not yet lay claim to the title of "Christian." They are progressively being saved on the nonlinear timetable of a higher power and not by the clocks of the conservative churchgoer who might be disappointed to see some of them in Heaven. These are not people who decidedly or consciously have rejected the name, person, or work of Christ, though they may for any number of reasons deny an association with a church or modern Christianity. I am talking about people who are seeking God, as they understand God, to the best of their ability in a form that works for them in real life and real time. They seek a "version" of God who has either been introduced to them along the way by saints with attractive lifestyles, or who they believe has found them in the midst of their searching and placed them on a higher plane of living. This God, that responds to prayer, revels in worship, and reveals his true nature through contemplation of life, love, and literature is no less the same God that countless Christians claim to be theirs. This is the Alpha and Omega, the Beginning and the End, the Great Is, and Is To Come who will one day unite all who honestly seek God under the name that is above all names, the King, the Lord, and the Messiah—Jesus the Christ.

What would be so wrong with admitting that we may not know everything there is to know about God? What if most of what we think we know about God is wrong, regardless of what we think Scripture teaches us? How small would our world be if we persisted in thinking that all who believe in God should view him in the same light or call him by the same name at this point in eternity? Unity that is evident to all will come later, as will our understanding of eternal perspective, but for now our planet still reels from the tower of Babel episode and hears a thousand different languages, through hundreds of different-colored faces in countries separated by myriads of miles, cultures, and systems of government. Is it not possible that we may also have countless ways of relating to and coming to believe in the same God? I have come to believe that though there is only one way to God, Christ is the lamppost for all true spiritual understanding and experience. And this in light of the fact that I don't know anyone who really understands God. As I was told in the early days of my sobriety when I was trying to find a way back to faith, there are only two things I really need to know about God for him to work in my life: 1) There is one, and 2) I am not him. So far, this is working quite a bit better for me than the jolly white giant and his two brothers. And on a personal level, this works way better than having it all figured out and judging everybody who doesn't believe as I do. I am lining up closer to where my friend Bruce is these days when he says, "The more I know, the less I know I know." Know what I mean?

# (28)

# LISTENING

## TRUE CONTEMPLATION
### *or the*
## DOG *and* PONY SHOW

His appearance changed from the inside out, right before their eyes. Sunlight poured from his face. . . . a light-radiant cloud enveloped them, and sounding from deep in the cloud a voice: "This is my Son, marked by my love, focus of my delight. Listen to him."

**Matthew 17:2, 5**
*The Message*

igh on an unnamed, Middle-Eastern mountain with his closest disciples, Peter, James, and John, Jesus Christ allowed a glimpse of his heavenly glory to shine through his earthly temple. Anyone who believes Christ to be merely a great teacher has obviously missed this Scripture account. Here, in Matthew's report of the event commonly referred to as the transfiguration, we see Christ changed "right before their eyes," leaving no doubt to any daring to pay attention to his eternal nature. The above descriptive narrative from Eugene Peterson's translation of the New Testament paints a picture of the Son of God wearing an outfit of human flesh with the glow of his deity radiating through. This, one of the few times that Christ overtly exposed his divinity beyond his human frame, most certainly left his three nearest followers in a state of astonishment. Though Jesus consistently tried to help his disciples to see beyond temporal constraints and into the realm of the unseen, they always seemed to be caught off guard whenever he showed them heavenly stuff. My guess is that they were so attached to their theories and fantasies of a Rome-bucking king and kingdom there just wasn't any room in their heads for matters concerning an invisible dimension with a culturally deviant operating system. I guess believing that Christ is God has always been a tough sell.

After the shock of this unexpected God scene began to wear off, Peter saw that Jesus was talking important things over with Moses and Elijah, two heavy-hitting Hebrew patriarchs. An impressive gathering to say the least, it is not clear why these two were chosen for this earthly visit with Christ. (I wonder what Abraham, Jacob, or even David thought when they learned they had not been invited to this powwow.) Regardless, the ever-emotional and impetuous Peter heard himself announcing aloud his impertinent plans for the immediate construction of what must have sounded to those present like three circus tents to mark this holy reunion. ("We'll have some fig wine, a few healed lepers, and maybe even a belly dancer or two!") But, while Peter's words still hung in the air like those in a cartoon conversation bubble, the booming voice of the Father God broke in from overhead to remind everyone that his Son, Jesus Christ, is the one true, chosen tabernacle and the preferred vehicle for delivering God's message of love to all mankind. Though Elijah and Moses had certainly played important roles in the mysterious lineage of grace and many righteous sayings had been attributed to them, it was the words and life of Christ that were to be heard far above and beyond all others. "This is my Son," the God voice bellowed from the cloud. "Hear ye him!"

God's voice spoke aloud in a similar way at Jesus' baptism (Matthew 3:17). There can be no doubt that God was sending a clear message to any present that day and to all who would later read about it. The Father was not just watching the back of his Son in a brawl for authority, he was revealing how he would bring about soul transformation for the common man—the transfiguration of any heart who truly desires change and is willing to go to any lengths to get it. "Listen to him" is not only a command given to the disciples who happened to be present during the short, earthly walk of Jesus. "Listen" is a method God prescribes for all who would live and learn the higher ways of God.

It's interesting that the verb God used here to describe our part in the partnership of spiritual change was not *study*, *strive*, *solve*, or even *sacrifice*, but *listen*. This ranks right up there on the scale of important messages with Christ's profound one-word admonitions to "seek," "knock," "ask," "pray," "give," "believe," "love," and "rest." Active verbs to be certain, but quiet, soft words that imply our miniscule effort will be met at the door of willingness by the power of God. And God will finish the miraculous assignment at hand and bring about the inner change that can only come through spiritual rearrangement. Our business is simply to humbly place ourselves, as best we know how, in a position where we can hear what he wants to tell us. This invaluable instruction delivered on the unnamed mountain by the Father himself may very well be the most profound counsel recorded in Scripture. Listen, for Christ's sake. It's a good beginning.

At the point when God interrupted the transfiguration party to straighten everyone out on who it was they were to listen to, Peter's grand idea for turning the mountain into a tabernacle construction site must have sounded like he had suggested making early reservations for a dog and pony show on Palm Sunday. His words just hadn't come out right. This was no surprise to any who knew Peter, for his reputation preceded him. He was the speak first, think later disciple. In time, he would add to his list of manic miscues the infamous "Let me come to you on the water"/"Help me, Lord, I'm drowning" incident, one I'm sure got him a lifetime of jabs from his fellow fishermen. Lucky for Peter, however, Jesus was not hung up on his imperfections and, much to his surprise, had great plans for him, including the "keys of the kingdom" job with the "on this rock I will build my church" designation (Matthew 16:18, 19). Peter's knack for not getting it right, and just plain not getting it, ironically made him the top choice to be the lead spokesman after Jesus' death, resurrection, and ascension. Another salvaged bad guy, the apostle Paul, also found himself in a leadership position in the early church in spite of his self-applied moniker, "chief of sinners." This is good news. It means there is hope for the run-of-the-mill, regular sinners like you and me. And while we are more likely these days to be preoccupied with building grand church structures than huts honoring those of our spiritual heritage, it is apparent that God will not abandon us for our inability to get it right or for failing to understand the true relevance of his visits to our little world.

For those of us who have made an art of proclaiming good intentions ("I am quitting smoking!" or "No more trips to the casino for me!") but have established a reputation for failing to keep our word ("Hey, didn't I see you chain-smoking at the casino?"), the apostle Peter is our poster man for change. In his life, we see that failures and faux pas in the hands of a loving God are nothing more than part of the process of growing up in Christ. It is apparently expected, in the big picture from God's-eye view, that we will falter and fall before finding a strong faith that can move mountains, one for which we would willingly die (or better yet, live). Our mistakes and inability to get it right are the very tools God uses for rebuilding our broken soulful natures, shaping them into colorful vessels of grace that can hold our adventurous stories of redemption. True disciples of Jesus are those who have been forced by their own blemished humanity to surrender and rely on the perfection and righteousness of Christ. This is the message of Christianity. The path by which Christ-followers have always grown in their God dependence has wound its way, twisting and turning, through valleys and shadows filled with reminders of their weaknesses and marked by signposts of their unfaithfulness. Our worst sin (or best, depending on your perspective) is often the very thing that prepares us for real and lasting change.

Too bad this process of surrender has to be so slow. Apparently, the supernatural quick-change stuff that occurs overnight, often including smoke, fire, and light, seems to have been reserved for a few special cases. For most of us, however, real change takes real time. Every person I know who has sought transformation at a serious and persistent level has been taught patience and learned obedience by the slow-moving influence of the Holy Spirit. Since all time is present to God, he is not in a hurry. Fortunately, grace and forgiveness are instant to those who believe and ever-present to those who seek them, allowing us unlimited and eternal relief from our worst-case selves. But the stuff of character adjustment, that which makes us incapable of continuing on the course of our old ways, is exceptional and requires much time and effort to achieve. This process of becoming holy is also known as *sanctification*, a word that, in itself, sounds tedious and time consuming. It would seem that God knows that changes occurring slowly over significant periods of Earth time are more likely to be permanent and leave us tasting better in the process.

Even though I have experienced noteworthy divine intervention more than once in my life, it has taken me years to get to the place where I don't create new and interesting ways of making myself and those around me miserable. It is no small God-doing that I don't tick someone off every single day and, in turn, get myself in a knot over someone else's mood or behavior. Neither my parents nor society is to blame for my tendency toward slow progress, as I was given much good and helpful information from an early age. The problem with me is that I have always known the right thing to do but have lacked the power to do it. I am one of those people who prefer schooling the hard way. And while there are some downsides to this method and pace of education, one of the upsides is that lessons learned like this are not soon forgotten. Self-reliance soon loses its luster when looking at another black eye in the mirror.

Perhaps the hardest part of my spiritual upbringing has been the process of learning to listen to God as he has chosen to speak to me. This continues to be a challenge, which I have accepted as part of the daily regimen of maintaining a spiritual awakening. Having been born with a Type A personality and a temperament that makes me prone to lead, I have a tendency to want to move fast and accomplish numerous tasks at once. I have even tried to multitask my devotional quiet times. Sitting still long enough to garner inspiration and receive direction from the Spirit has been a slow-coming, acquired ability. Since developing a taste for contemplative listening and living, however, the thought of going back to life without it seems intolerable. Upon discovering that life in the slow lane affords a more enjoyable and healthy pace as well as a much better view, I have become willing to pull over and let the world pass me by at its preferred breakneck speed. There is no law that says I must live my life at 10 mph over the speed limit like everyone else, just as there is no guarantee that those who get there quicker, wherever "there" is, will enjoy life more. On the contrary, the real trick to finding contentment comes in living to the fullest the life I currently lead rather than rushing about in search of a better one. This is why I am taking to heart the resounding God words cast down from the sky on that memorable day sometime around AD 31. Listening to Christ, as he would reveal himself to me, is my best solution for feeling comfortable in my own skin, as well as getting along with others in this world—regardless of the speed they choose to travel. And as you can probably tell, I am not one who believes there is any shortage of how Christ can and will speak to us if we daily open our hearts, eyes, and ears to meet him on a mountain, in the silence, or even in a dog and pony show.

# (29)

# OPEN-
# MINDEDNESS

## of HURRICANES and HAPPENSTANCE

As I lived under the Cross and simply followed the openings of Truth, my mind from day to day was more enlightened; my former acquaintance was left to judge of me as they would, for I found it safest for me to live in private and keep these things sealed up in my own breast. While I silently ponder on that change wrought in me, I find no language equal to it nor any means to convey to another a clear idea of it. I looked upon the works of God in this visible creation and an awfulness covered me; my heart was tender and often contrite, and a universal love to my fellow creatures increased in me. This will be understood by such as have trodden in the same path.

**John Woolman**
From *Quaker Spirituality: Selected Writings*,
edited by Douglas V. Steere

Water stood a foot deep in the yard and covered the road in front of our house, but that didn't stop sightseers and local four-wheelers from driving back and forth, like kids riding their bikes through thunderstorm mud puddles. Two days after Hurricane Alex shook our cottage and flooded our North Carolina barrier island, I was finally able to walk to the beach and see the aftermath of the storm that no one took seriously until it was on top of us. The sea was still swollen and churning with passive-aggressive anger and at the base of the dunes, debris that beachcombers don't usually stumble across littered the beach: a set of stairs, a boat battery, a whole cedar tree, a roll of fence, and various other chunks of trash, shells, seaweed, and lumber. Compressed by powerful waves and a storm surge that had carried multiple billions of gallons of seawater well past the normal high-tide line, the sand was surprisingly flat; the suntanned beach, long and wide, was as smooth as a freshly sanded table. An unusual sight for August, not a fishing boat could be spotted; their captains wisely leery of the choppy seas and deadly riptides that typically accompany a hurricane. Many landlubbers take the fury of nature lightly but those who make their living from the sea are hard to fool.

As I walked the compacted beach at sunup, I recalled that each morning of life is a blank page thirsty for the ink of honest and inspired words, an empty canvas awaiting the colors and brushstrokes of a new creation. The mind open to the will and ways of God, however and whenever God chooses to reveal them, is like a ship exploring uninhabited islands on uncharted seas. Compulsive questions of how? where? why? and when? are drowned out by the trumpeted joys of redemption. Whether a steadfast believer or a faith-touched doubter, the man or woman at the helm of this surrendered mind can press his or her face into the misty breezes of unknown goodness and taste the honeyed anticipation of happiness and worth. God is the captain of this vessel, and there is nothing on this voyage to fear or regret but fear and regret. Though storms of alarm and dread or winds of lethargy and apathy may have rocked your recent days or months, there on the sun-streaked horizon lies the hope of something different, something new, and something better. This daybreak of the human spirit is the finite point in time where a new beginning is but a fresh embrace of the eternal present where God lives. In the expanse of a mind open to the powers and visions of God there is no end to the brightness ahead and no bottom to the chasms of his mercy and grace.

Before I sobered up from alcoholism in 1989 through a much-needed indoctrination into a 12-step way of life, I used to wonder why God would not answer my desperate prayers for continuous sobriety. Though I had survived a divine intervention in my teenage years, I misunderstood God's continuing process of sanctification. I wanted to be holy, but on my terms. As I would soon discover, God just doesn't work that way. Having seen the white light of a spiritual awakening and having had a sudden change in attitude and temperament, I wrongly assumed that with a little prayer and Bible study (and a ministry degree from a Christian university to boot), I would enjoy an effortless coast through life and on into Heaven. In spite of much exposure to godly influence, I failed to see that to continue in the grace of my deliverance I would need to enlarge my spiritual life on a regular basis; ego, fear, and pride would need to be surrendered at the deepest levels. Substituting religious activity for devotion and selflessness I found my soul eerily vacant and prone to spiritual decline, as in the parable of the man repossessed by unclean spirits (Matthew 12:43-45). No wonder that my relapses into drugs and alcohol—in spite of much prayer and struggle to resist—became increasingly worse and more frequent, forcing me to leave my home and ministry out of guilt and despair. Four years, three treatment centers, two short ministries, and one divorce later, I finally made a decision to let God decide what I needed to do in order to cease this pattern of self-destruction and become usefully whole. My prescription for how God should work in my life had failed.

Fortunately, my years of rebellion and frustration were not wasted, for as with Jonah, the whale of desperation spit me upon the shores of willingness along with the precious gift of an open mind. On this date, August 22, 1989, I let go of the reigns of my life and began my journey of letting God show me the way to go home. It had never occurred to me prior to that day that though I had been awash in spiritual intentions and had articulated my religious convictions in earnest, my closed-mindedness to new truth had limited God's ability to complete my transformation. So it was, with no fanfare announcing my surrender and no celebrated battlefield upon which to lay my sword, I silently and completely relinquished my will and mind to the heart of God. Ironically, I felt a sense of great freedom in the knowledge that I possessed no power to change my situation or alter my own direction. Of my own, I was nothing. I would have to trust God for everything, including the first steps to this new beginning. With hope and confidence, I leaned into this storied faith that I had preached about but had never lived. In utter reliance upon things unseen, I admitted my need for a power greater than all that I knew or understood to relieve me of the bondage of self and to take me beyond where I had been able to go on my own resources. I needed God for my next breath. I needed God for the courage to change. I needed God for the ability to need God—and God was there waiting, delighted by it all.

While there was no flash of light or sudden release as I had experienced a decade before, I was somehow filled with an awareness that someone was going to take care of me and in fact, had been doing so for a long time. Like the miraculous parting of the Red Sea, held back by gargantuan invisible hands, my mind was pried open to possibilities for recovery and life beyond my ability to comprehend them. In the days and weeks that followed, the perpetual black pillar of despair that had accompanied me for years dissipated as I threw myself into the faith-filled fellowship of recovering alcoholics. No longer would I harbor any serious objections or reservations, though from time to time some would cross my mind. From that day forward I would follow, though often blindly and full of doubt, wherever God would lead, and do whatever would be required of me to become a vessel of his love and grace. Although I had once been afraid of it and had almost thrown my life away to avoid it, this Spirit course would in time lead me into practicing time-tested biblical principles of surrender, faith, honesty, confession, obedience, restitution, community, unconditional love, forgiveness, prayer, meditation, and, every once in a while, sacrificial service to others. Every day, one day at a time, since 1989, I have followed this path of open-mindedness, amazed and humbled by its effectiveness in keeping me in favor with God and man.

One night, shortly before moving away from Hatteras Island for the second time, I walked to the ocean to listen to the roar of the edge of the world. As those lucky enough to live beyond the light-polluted skies of a city can attest, nothing can reveal to you the reality of your proper size on this planet like a gaze into the starry night sky. Humility comes easily to a face full of Milky Way. One of the things I have loved about living near the ocean, in spite of the wild weather and the endless tourist traffic, is the clean, salty-sweet air that greets you whenever you step outside. Breathing in and out, focusing on taking in God's good, and releasing my self-centered anxieties, these raw scents sweep through your nasal passages like the aromas of popcorn and cotton candy at a state fair, making it impossible to dwell on unhappy or negative thoughts. Just as you rarely see someone frowning while riding a merry-go-round, a brisk walk makes it difficult to hold onto harsh ideas. No matter what burdens I may drag through the day, I can count on finding a clear head and an open mind while strolling down a wide-open beach, through a farmer's field, on a wooded trail, or in a neighborhood park where deep breaths and intentional mutterings to God lead me back to a level of friendship with my Creator that I enjoyed in childhood.

This touch from God through open-mindedness requires a childlike faith difficult for the intellectually mature adult to uncover. But it's down there somewhere, at the bottom of a pile of concerns and possessions, waiting to make our acquaintance and lead us into ordinary and extraordinary touches of the divine. To say yes to a life beyond the confines of the human understanding is to stand on the shoulders of the likes of recently fabled outdoorsman, Aron Ralston (who cut off his own hand to save his life)—high atop the peaks of his Colorado fourteeners, glimpsing life beyond the treacherous, surmounted, and fathomable end. With a little imagination to see the character and hand of God in all things and situations, not only will everything always turn out to be all right on this journey of life, but there will also be revelations and jubilations beyond the boundaries of the human experience. This, I believe is the kingdom of Heaven we all seek.

# ( 30 )

# ART

## MOJO, MOMENTUM, *and the* LIGHT *of the* WORLD

Art work is ordinary work, but it takes courage to embrace that work, and wisdom to mediate the interplay of art and fear. Sometimes to see your work's rightful place you have to walk to the edge of the precipice and search the deep chasms. You have to see that the universe is not formless and dark throughout, but awaits simply the revealing light of your own mind. Your art does not arrive miraculously from the darkness, but is made uneventfully in the light.

**David Bayles and Ted Orland**
*Art & Fear:*
*Observations on the Perils (and Rewards) of Artmaking*

A s all artists discover in due time, inspiration or the muse can often be fleeting, even elusive. While I have been fortunate enough to experience seasons of creativity that arrived seemingly without effort, I have learned that if I want to be an artist with a capital *A*, I must live a lifestyle that is conducive to creativity. Like the Spirit of God which blows this way and that and comes and goes as he chooses, the spirit of creativity may drop in for a whimsical visit from time to time, but it must be welcomed and nurtured for it to become a permanent resident in the heart of the seeker. The pursuit of creativity, much like that of spiritual growth, must be more than the occasional voyeuristic participation in a God-gathering. It is a daily discipline that reaches beyond the analytical mind and down into the dark side of the soul for that next sweaty rung on the ladder of faith. Creative adventure, as with spiritual expansion, requires effort. It is hard work, but the pay is out of this world.

In my search to keep the artistic channels open and my spirit moving in the direction of imaginative enlargement, I have identified some basic principles that in addition to keeping me healthy and happy, enable frequent touches from the hand of the Creator himself.

## Simplicity

Keeping life uncluttered is an essential ingredient to the process of creativity. This is not always about the limitation or elimination of tangible, material things. Often the substance that clutters my artistic mind is not an actual possession but merely a thought or a concern surrounding the acquisition or maintenance of one. As the apostle Paul wrote to Timothy, it is not money but "the love of money [that] is a root of all kinds of evil" (1 Timothy 6:10). Possessions are not inherently bad, and money by itself has no power to do harm. However, without a plethora of noisy TVs, toys, games, vehicles, and communication devices to distract and entertain me, I am more inclined to notice and respond when the urge to create comes calling. Often this arrives as a still, small voice that I may not notice if I am surrounded by sound and activity. Noise—even a steady stream of religious music—can be a logjam in the river of creative silence.

## Prayer and meditation

I must invite the great Creator into my life on a daily basis to have a chance at continuity in any creative endeavor. I can do most things once, or for a day, on my own power, but I will eventually run out of steam unless I am frequently plugged into my divine power source. Here is where creativity and spirituality become kissing cousins. When I keep the ears of my heart open to the voice of God through a devotional and contemplative lifestyle, not only do I walk in God's will (in spite of frequent human error), but I am cut loose from fear and freed to drift, yea swim, in the rivers of creation. Here, I touch the hem of the holy garment and am blessed to be in like mind with the ultimate designer, and in league with the very Spirit responsible for all that has been and will ever be created.

## Exercise

Taking long walks or bicycle rides moves my blood around and opens the valves and vessels of my heart and lungs to the oxygen of new experience. Soaking in God's nature, basking in the gifts of movable arms and legs, gives me gratitude and life from which to draw when I sit in front of a blank canvas, paper, or computer screen. On many occasions, I have written my way through a particular foggy place in a story after taking a brisk stroll around the block.

This physical act of exertion loosens the grip that my mind sometimes has on a project, allowing the other side (the right side) of my brain to inject fresh enthusiasm and thoughts into what has become a stagnant puddle of old ideas.

## Availability

I once read an interview with Paul McCartney in which he said that his key to writing a song was many times as simple as having an instrument in his hand. This has also been true for me, as I can get inspired to write songs simply by sitting around, fiddling with my guitar. Oftentimes, I do not know the subject of my painting until long after I have picked up the paints and brushes, working with anticipation to see what unfolds before me. The muse, that mythical quality or character that all artists and writers know can take them to a place beyond their own ability to create, is perhaps, in me, nothing more than the childlike nature of the Holy Spirit. This elusive influence most often surfaces in my studio when I exhibit the willingness to work simply by starting. Waiting to be inspired leads to much inspired waiting.

## Books, art, movies, and music

Exposure to the creative birthings of other people sometimes shakes me out of a slump and gives me the proverbial shot in the arm I need to begin my art again. I love to read journals and biographies of artists and musicians, not so much for the instructional value, but to see how they lived; what lengths they traveled and what sacrifices they made for their craft. Sadly, the dead artists, particularly the ones who died young and tragically, always seem to be the most interesting and certainly sell the most copies. The short lives of Basquiat, Van Gogh, Pollock, and others have not been wasted if their influence leads people to pick up the tools of their craft and create something new and fresh.

I also love watching movies, particularly since I killed my television in 1995. I get a mental buzz, sort of an escapist high, from films, but I also garner artistic inspiration from them. The stranger the movie, the more surprising the plot, the better it seems to affect me. As violence and sex are often fillers for inferior screenplays or storylines, I have noticed that the best films don't contain much of either. On the other hand, some of the most creative movies seem to have a plethora of what would be called foul language. For some reason this does not bother me, though I am very aware of how much it bothers many of my fellow Christ-followers. I can't explain it, but I've learned not to look in the mouth of the gift horse that starts my creative juices flowing. All I know is that it is not unusual for me to start and finish a painting or write a chapter for a book late at night after having watched a film earlier in the evening. Fortunately, if we wade through most of the muck coming out of Hollywood these days, we find that there is no shortage of great films, foreign and domestic, springing from the creative pool of writers and directors who desire to make something beautiful and possibly meaningful while they walk this planet.

## The streak

When the art touch from God is on my shoulders and I am walking with a whistle on my lips like Uncle Remus and his zip-a-dee-doo-dah bluebird, I have found it to be important to ride the momentum and resist the temptation to rest on my laurels. In sports, the winning streak is revered and protected, even by superstitious practices like not changing dirty socks or not shaving until the team loses. I know that when I have a good round of golf going, I am hesitant to spit out my gum or take a drink of water if I think it will monkey with my mojo. In my little world I have discovered that creativity breeds creativity and, knowing how hard it is sometimes to get it all started, it would not be inappropriate for an artist to protect a streak at any reasonable cost. This might include extreme measures such as not stopping to eat, ignoring the ringing phone, or even taking the batteries out of the clock if these will prolong in any way the mood and mode of creativity in process.

Reasonable to one person might be perceived as outrageous or immature to another, and each artist will have to make that call individually. On more than one occasion, I have been willing to quit a job or move to a different house or even another state when it became apparent that this was necessary for me to keep uncovered the light of Christ and the truth about who he is making me. Christ said,

> You are the light of the world. A city on a hill cannot be hidden. Neither do people light a lamp and put it under a bowl. Instead they put it on its stand, and it gives light to everyone in the house. In the same way, let your light shine before men, that they may see your good deeds and praise your Father in heaven. (Matthew 5:14-16)

As David Bayles and Ted Orland said, art "does not arrive miraculously from the darkness, but is made uneventfully in the light." It is the stuff of the everyday man and woman who would seek God in the creative and the contemplative. Quakers wait together in a fellowship of silence for the inner light of Christ to reveal more of who he is and more of who we are becoming in him. Artists, writers, musicians, and the like all know that waiting on this light of creation doesn't always mean sitting in silence until the muse chooses to materialize. Sometimes, with a heart full of faith and a spirit of adventure, one has to go out and find the point of inspired departure by stepping up to the canvas, the paper, or the instrument and letting it fly.

This is the path of God-seeking that never leaves the seeker wanting or dissatisfied. This is the road to righteousness that is paved with freedom, color, beauty, and sound. And this journey into the Spirit is not limited to those who would be artists with a capital *A*, but is available to any and all who would trust the process and make the choices necessary for its incarnation. For all I know, the artistic endeavors that draw me like a moth to the flame and burn from me like a blazing beacon may be the most honest expressions of God's touch on my life. Ever. As in the parables of the pearl of great price and the treasure hidden in a field, I am selling all I have to place myself under the influence of this particular God touch. And nothing gives me greater joy than to share it with others. "Hide it under a bushel? No! I'm gonna let it shine." Wanna join me?

# NOT THE END

Thank you for sharing my spiritual journey with me by taking the time to read this book. If you would like to dialogue with me regarding your journey, I would be interested in hearing from you. Please send your e-mail comments to me via dangilliam@earthlink.net or by letter through the publisher. You can also track more of my creative pilgrimage through the original music and paintings available at www.dangilliam.net. When visiting the Web site, don't forget to sign up to receive e-mail updates from me regarding future articles, books, art, and music. Presently I am working on my second book, which is a work of historical fiction called *The Journals of Jesus*. Stay tuned and seek God. He is making us all more of who he wants us to be.